**An Exhibition of Books
and Manuscripts**

April 10 - July 12, 1989

Louis R. Lurie Rotunda
Cecil H. Green Library

First Drafts, Last Drafts

Forty Years of the
Creative Writing Program
at Stanford

Prepared by
William McPheron

with the assistance of
Amor Towles

Preface by
John L'Heureux

Stanford University Libraries
Stanford California
1989

ISBN 0-911221-12-3

Contents

Acknowledgments

It is with special pleasure that the University Libraries take note of the remarkable talents brought together annually for more than forty years by Stanford's Creative Writing Program. The distinguished writers whose achievements are the subjects of this exhibit amply illustrate the range, diversity, and quality of a program that has, as John L'Heureux notes, resisted becoming a "school." Documenting the pluralism of the Writing Program, capturing its variety, suggesting its vitality, and freezing momentarily the uniqueness of its creativity have been some of the aims of this show. If the Writing Program as a whole can be seen as a sort of library of mid-twentieth-century American fiction and verse, this exhibit points to the archive behind that library, the intimate record of art in process. William McPheron, the Libraries' Curator of British and American Literature, has done a masterful job in coordinating this complex show, and his sensitive essays sustain an engagement with the material that points to a deeper involvement with writing—and reading. Amor Towles ably assisted with research and preparation of the catalogue.

To the twenty writers who have not only lent material for the show but contributed their reflections as well, the Libraries are deeply grateful and appreciative. This exhibit is their exhibit: their guidance, comments, and counsel have been integral to it from the start. Special thanks are owed to Tess Gallagher, who handled Raymond Carver's part in the show during his last illness and after his untimely death. John L'Heureux's advice in planning and assistance in organizing the exhibit were indispensable, and his enthusiasm for the project was reassuring from the start. Other libraries were generous in lending us material: the Harry Ransom Humanities Research Center at the University of Texas, Austin; the University of Houston; and the library of the State University of New York at Buffalo. John Leggett graciously allowed us to reproduce selections of his correspondence with Larry McMurtry.

Publication of this catalogue was made possible by the William K. Glikbarg Fund, which has played such a central role in allowing the Libraries to bring their exhibits to a wider audience.

Michael T. Ryan

Frances and Charles Field Curator of Special Collections and Director of Library Collections

Preface

Apart from their eminence as literary figures, these twenty writers have only one thing in common. Not style or substance, not the measure of a line of poetry or the strategies of a short story, not attitude or belief or unbelief. What they have in common is this: at a significant moment in their development as writers, each of them participated in the Stanford Writing Workshop. This exhibit celebrates these writers individually and as a group and it testifies to the workshop's success in fostering the development of personal talent, voice, vision.

The writing workshop is a relatively recent phenomenon. When Wallace Stegner founded the Stanford Writing Workshop in 1946, it was—after Iowa—the second degree-granting program in the country. Over the years, Stanford and Iowa have maintained their primacy of place, and do so still, even as writing programs proliferate around them. Indeed, today more than 300 other programs graduate from 7000 to 8000 writers each year. The effect has been interesting, or, from another point of view, devastating. The level of performance by students in writing programs has risen palpably—because after all one can learn *craft*—but there is less and less opportunity for true genius to assert itself and to catch notice. Fiction and poetry are being smothered beneath a landslide of competence.

It goes without saying that not all workshops succeed and when they fail, they fail in different ways. A workshop fails when it produces writers who write like each other or, more often the case, write like the workshop leader. A workshop fails when its graduates produce poems and stories that are perfect examples of craft but are not animated by the life and fire of talent. A workshop fails when it lays down rules, becomes prescriptive or proscriptive, forces the individual talent into a form it does not want and cannot fill. A workshop fails when it exalts mediocrity and ignores excellence so that everybody can feel equal and nobody will feel bad. A workshop fails when it praises too much, praises too little, substitutes praise for criticism. As it is in life, so it is in workshop: there are a thousand ways to fail.

A workshop succeeds when it empowers writers, when it helps them tap their energy and imagination, when it gives them access to their deepest and richest material and urges them to see it with the clarity and strength that only they possess. A workshop succeeds *fully* when its writers summon their strongest material, exploit it for its power and pain and humor and humanity, animate it with the sound of a personal and particularized voice, illuminate it with the hard pure light of artistic vision. The poem or story, then, is theirs: uniquely, unforgettably, a work of art.

But success or failure, the workshop—as a part of the creative process—remains mysterious to the larger number of us. Let me address the mystery of the writing workshop itself: what it is, what goes on there, why, and to what end.

Historically, the workshop filled the gap left by two vanished institutions: the Patron who provided the artist with time and money; the Editor who guided the writer with good counsel and assisted at the birth of the artwork. But the Medicis are gone and the Max Perkinses are rare indeed. They have been replaced, however inadequately, by hundreds of writing workshops.

In my fiction workshop, a fairly typical one, twelve people sit at a long table and listen while somebody reads a new and therefore fragile piece of fiction. After the reading, the eleven others discuss the story, frankly and sometimes brutally, as if the author weren't sitting there with them. They talk about what the story is trying to do, how it's trying to do it, whether it has used the best means to the desired end, and how well the story succeeds. I sit at one end of the table, the dread thirteenth person, and try to say as little as possible. Occasionally I interrupt with a question or a comment that is meant to steer the discussion toward the larger and more important issues. At the end, I summarize, hitting the major points and leaving the rest for a written report I give to the author. When the workshop meeting goes well, we succeed in creating a kind of critical essay on the story at hand, everybody is satisfied, and the author goes away with a clear sense of how to revise the story to achieve the symmetry and perfection it deserves. When the workshop doesn't go well, nobody feels satisfied, the author goes away hurt and depressed and sometimes vengeful, and I wonder why I didn't become a painter like my father.

What I've described here is the ideal workshop meeting, and it's pretty rare; as rare, I imagine, as the total disaster. Most workshop meetings are neither miraculous nor hellish. They're located somewhere in between—in a place where comments do not build on one another to form a shapely and intelligent critical essay but stumble over one another in contradiction, exclamation, and often laughter; where I talk altogether too much; where the writer, filled with pride of authorship and blindly defensive, protests against any and all criticism; where one or two comments are meant less to enlighten than to retaliate for what was said last week; where the participants feel they were not nearly so helpful as they might have been; and where the author goes away with a pretty good sense of how to make the story work *despite* what everybody said.

A writing workshop, even the best, is wanton with energy and talent; it can crush the weak and empower the crass; it offers endless opportunity to give and receive injury; it is frequently as frustrating, indeed as maddening, as life itself. Surely the writing workshop is the oddest, most problematic, most dangerous, and least economical route to take on the way to becoming a writer. And yet all the poets and fiction writers in this exhibit have taken exactly that route.

They have done so because, when all the bad things about it have been said, the writing workshop finally is the one place where you can be sure you and your work are taken seriously, where your writing intentions are honored, where even in a mean-spirited comment you can divine—if you wish—the truth about your writing, its strengths and its weaknesses. It is a place where you are surrounded by people whose chief interest in life is also yours, where the talk is never anything but writing and writing well and writing better, where book chat is the primitive and calculating talk of writers rather than the civil and judiciary talk of critics, where money is always short but somehow someone always has the latest Carver or Paley or Updike and it's passed around and admired and responded to. It is where they give you a little time and a little money and a lot of emotional and psychological support. It is where somehow you pick up the notion that what you're doing is a good and noble thing, and though you may not write as well as you'd like, it is enough and will suffice.

Which brings me full circle to this writing program, this exhibit, these writers. What they have in common is the Stanford Writing Workshop, where they developed a talent and a voice and a vision unique to each of them. Where they began a career we see documented in this exhibit. And where they achieved a sense of excellence that will suffice. And will survive.

John L'Heureux

Director
Creative Writing Program
Melvin and Bill Lane Professor in the Humanities

Introduction

The twenty writers featured in this exhibit and catalog are linked both by their importance to contemporary American letters and by their association with Stanford's Creative Writing Program. To highlight their prominence on today's literary scene, a tally could easily be made of the Pulitzer Prizes, American Book Awards, Guggenheim Fellowships, and other honors the group has received over the past forty years. Though this would certainly be a reliable index of collective success, it would also distract from the individuality of the writers' achievements and obscure the unique trajectories of their creative lives. And precisely this singularity of style and accomplishment is what emerges most forcefully from the manuscripts and personal statements gathered here.

The manuscripts, in particular, are eloquent declarations of each writer's distinctive temperament. Many of them reflect poetry and fiction that was conceived during the author's time at Stanford; others document the composition of more recent pieces. What all these working papers offer is an intimate view of the creative process, and taken together they cast much light on the difficult course of literature's evolution from initiating gesture to achieved form. But to examine these manuscripts for clues about how the literary mind operates is soon to conclude that generalization is almost impossible.

A few authors—Philip Levine in poetry and Al Young in fiction offer interesting examples—sometimes begin and end fluently, writing confidently and revising only minimally before reaching their final drafts. More common is the slow, layered development of a piece through numerous complete drafts, each subtly reshaping the originating impulse. Instructive models here are Evan S. Connell's complicated construction of his study of General George Armstrong Custer and Robert Pinsky's gradual transformation of a Biblical psalm into a contemporary religious meditation. Even within this pattern of incremental buildup, there are notable differences in manner and pace. Raymond Carver, whose scrupulous sense of craft typically forces a story through a dozen or more drafts, nonetheless often proceeds by sudden bursts, advancing steadily across long stretches of text before inspiration wanes or knotty cruxes develop. In contrast, Alan Shapiro tends to roughly sketch large blocks of his dramatic monologues and then move forward by concentrating intensely on single lines, working deliberately through one variation after the other.

The writers' strategies for revision are as informative as their general habits of composition. Revision can proceed by the addition of new materials, by the deletion of previously drafted passages, or by discrete changes to the existing text. Sometimes revision is integral to the act of writing, occurring simultaneously with the draft at hand. More often, it takes place later, the lapse of time bringing into focus the need for rewriting. A remarkable instance of this practice is Donald Justice's multiple reworkings of a single manuscript draft, each pass made in a different color of ink and then carefully dated. Another approach shared by several writers is exemplified by Harriet Doerr's method of flagging passages that she intends to return to later. Here the author immediately recognizes the necessity for further attention but defers the task to subsequent drafts.

The revision process usually extends over weeks or months, but sometimes much longer periods must pass before the work finds a shape that satisfies the writer. Donald Hall was still altering his celebration of his son's birth years after the poem appeared in print, while Wendell Berry made major changes in the conclusion of *Nathan Coulter* when this first novel was reprinted almost three decades after its original publication. Also important in the context of revision is the role of agents and publishers, whose calls for change can significantly affect a work. Ernest J. Gaines testifies to the beneficence of his agent's editorial hand, and the final structure of Al Young's first novel, *Snakes,* owes much to the insight of a helpful editor. But the relation between writer and editor can also become a battle of wills, pushing the piece in directions that ultimately displease the author. Larry McMurtry's struggle with his editor at Harper & Row over *Horseman, Pass By* provides a vivid instance of such conflict.

Considered from the perspective of aesthetic form, the manuscripts reveal a daunting range of evolutionary possibilities. Some works—like Thom Gunn's poetic treatment of California motorcyclists in "On the Move"—are governed from the beginning by abstract ideas. Others, like N. Scott Momaday's lyric projection of American Indian ritual, originate in a single powerful image and only later discover their organizing principle. Still other pieces spring from the challenge of artistic imitation, developing through highly self-conscious competition with literary forebears. A revealing example of this compositional model is Edgar Bowers's "Thirteen Views of Santa Barbara," which draws on traditions in both the visual arts and poetry. At a more technical level, structure sometimes precedes content and leads it forward, a pattern evident in the early drafts of Robert Hass's historical revery, "Palo Alto: The Marshes." But other times the work's controlling theme emerges imperceptibly from the definition of local details, a phenomenon Tobias Wolff candidly describes in his account of the genesis of his short story, "Coming Attractions."

Apparently mundane but, in fact, no less fascinating, is the variety of physical materials and tools the writers employ. The selection of notebook or loose paper and the size of each may seem inconsequential, but a consideration of Tillie Olsen's improvisational use of different formats of paper for different purposes tells much about the workings of her imagination. Also conspicuous among her papers—as well as in the manuscripts of many other writers here—is the significance frequently attached to the writing instrument itself, not only the preference for pencil, ball point or fountain pen but also the choice of lead or ink color. The change from one medium to another often marks a shift in artistic plan, signalling the intention to start afresh. Similarly, the writer's choice of longhand, typewriter, or more recently, a personal computer, is seldom arbitrary. Rather, each technology possesses its own distinct feel, and the decision about when to rely on which bears directly on the creative task at hand. This interactive relation between writing and its tools is evident in all the authors' work but is particularly intriguing in the cases of Scott Turow, whose novel, *Presumed Innocent,* moved from longhand notebooks to computer, and Tobias Wolff, who depends entirely on his computer, completely deleting all stages of his work prior to the final draft.

The act of writing encompasses, in short, a bewildering variety of factors. When these enter the field of each author's individual temperament, differences multiply into an astonishing range of unique configurations. Confronted by so much singularity, perhaps the best response is to marvel at how unpredictable and arduous are the routes the creative mind takes to its destination. The uncompromising search for effective form and expressive phrase, the fine discriminations of sense, rhythm, and sound, the ceaseless concern for clarity and precision—these efforts visibly trace themselves in the manuscripts and clearly announce the writers' shared commitment to perfecting their art.

Amid this abundance of literary achievement, the possibility of failure seems distant, and would have gone unvoiced were it not for Thomas McGuane. The audience he imagines staring into the exhibit's display cases consists of beginning writers, serious about their craft but still unpublished—in other words, just those young authors for whom the prospect of failure looms largest. As a gesture of assurance and encouragement to them, McGuane chose to ignore his years of success and focus instead on work from his own apprentice days. These manuscripts of early, unaccepted work offer consolation, for they frankly acknowledge the dead ends which even the most talented artists sometimes encounter.

The writers' personal statements complement their manuscripts. In addition to illuminating their work and methods, most recall the time at Stanford and assess its impact on their professional development. Perspectives here are as unique as habits of composition, but when taken together, they bear witness to the vitality of the literary community which for four decades has organized itself at Stanford around the Creative Writing Program. Each of the twenty writers benefited from the program, but their formal relations to it varied considerably. A number arrived on campus as doctoral students in English. For them, the workshops in poetry and fiction were outside their designated course of study, and they often attended independently. Several participated in the program as master's candidates in English with an emphasis in creative writing. Most, however, were Creative Writing Fellows, accomplished but unestablished authors who came to Stanford for a year as nonmatriculated students to sharpen their writing skills. For some time now, the fellowships granting this year of artistic grace have been named in honor of Wallace Stegner, the novelist, short story writer, and social historian who conceived the program in 1946.

Wallace Stegner had joined Stanford's faculty only the preceding year. Recruited from a Harvard instructorship in creative writing, he was appointed to succeed Edith Mirrielees, a quietly charismatic figure who for thirty-five years taught writing at Stanford. Mirrielees' specialty was fiction. During summers over a twenty-year span she handled the short story course at the famed Bread Loaf Writers' Conference in Vermont, and her *Writing the Short Story,* first published in 1929 and regularly revised in succeeding decades, was a standard handbook in the field. Fiction was Stegner's forte as well. Since 1939 he, too, had taught at Bread Loaf, where he and Mirrielees first became friends. And by the time Stanford attracted Stegner to campus with its offer of a full professorship in English, he had already published eight books, five of them novels, including the now classic *Big Rock Candy Mountain* (1943). Furthermore, Stegner knew firsthand the value of classroom stimulation to aspiring writers, since his own serious commitment to fiction dated from his student days with Norman Foerster at the University of Iowa's Writers Workshop.

So when Stegner walked into a Stanford classroom in the fall of 1945 and found a group of unusually gifted World War II veterans eager for literary instruction, he immediately realized "that the university had to provide for them something more than the routine writing course designed for eighteen-year-olds." Drawing on his own experience at Iowa, Bread Loaf, and Harvard, he drafted a comprehensive plan for financial support, regular workshops, annual prizes, and guest lectureships, all intended, in Stegner's words, to "make a literary career visible and credible and help young writers prepare for it." Before seeking funds from the University's general administration, he showed the proposal to the head of the English Department, Richard F. Jones. By good fortune, Professor Jones's brother, Dr. Edward H. Jones, "an M.D.," Stegner observes, "who liked literature better than medicine, and who owned Texas oil wells," offered to support the program for five years, a pledge that Dr. Jones soon converted into a permanent endowment.

Building on this foundation, Stanford's Creative Writing Program has developed steadily over the last forty years. Its intellectual and emotional center is the workshop, which meets twice a week to discuss participants' new work. Originally there were separate tracks for fiction, poetry, and drama, but playwriting was soon dropped. That occurred at the same time the yearly prizes were eliminated—experience having proven that the bad feeling engendered by competition outweighed the benefits. The decades have brought other changes. The numbers of both faculty and Stegner Fellows have increased; a bequest from Edith Mirrielees allowed broader support for M.A. candidates; Jones Lectureships in Creative Writing were established. These three-year, part-time teaching appointments, awarded to recent fellows, provide a job that enables them to keep their attention focused on writing.

Two other refinements in the program also deserve special mention. First, the Lane Lectures Series, endowed by Jean and Bill Lane, annually brings to campus several internationally famous authors who give a public reading and conduct a session of the writing workshops. Among these guests have been Donald Barthelme, Nadine Gordimer, Toni Morrison, Joyce Carol Oates, Eudora Welty, and Richard Wilbur. The Lane Lectures have also brought back to campus Stegner himself as well as four of the Program's students—Wendell Berry, Raymond Carver, Thom Gunn, and Larry McMurtry. Second, in 1990 the Creative Writing Program's commitment to nurturing professional authors will be strengthened by phasing out the M.A. option and concentrating exclusively on fellows, whose numbers will increase to ten each in fiction and poetry. This is a daring and innovative move that promises to inaugurate a new phase in Stanford's support of contemporary letters.

For the first twenty-five years, Stegner directed the program with the aid of his associate, Richard Scowcroft, a novelist and academic, whom Stegner brought to Stanford from Harvard. Stegner retired in 1971, the same year he published his Pulitzer Prize-winning novel, *Angle of Repose.* Scowcroft then assumed the administrative duties, a post he maintained until his own retirement in 1978. For the past decade, the director has been the novelist, short story writer, and poet John L'Heureux, who joined Stanford's faculty in 1973. As teachers, the three have been decisive in shaping the fiction workshops. In fact, in the Creative Writing Program's entire history, there have been only two other regular teachers of these advanced seminars—short story writer and memoirist Nancy Packer, whose involvement dates from her own Stegner Fellowship in 1959-60, and more recently, novelist, critic, and poet Gilbert Sorrentino, who came to Stanford in 1982. While this small core of permanent writing faculty has given the fiction workshops an enviable stability, a remarkable series of other authors have enlivened it with variety. Albert J. Guerard and Frank O'Connor taught for considerable periods and returned more than once as seminar leaders. Others have also given substantial time to the fiction workshops, including William Abrahams, Alice Adams, Hortense Calisher, Walter Van Tilburg Clark, Malcolm Cowley, Herbert Gold, Grace Paley, and Katherine Anne Porter, along with former Stegner Fellows Ernest J. Gaines, Tillie Olsen, and Robert Stone.

Stegner himself set the style—both aesthetic and pedagogical—that still governs the fiction workshops. His artistic roots lie deep in the tradition of literary realism created by such novelists as Mark Twain, William Dean Howells, Joseph Conrad, and Willa Cather. Stegner's personal inflection of this tradition is marked by a special reverence for what he calls "the company of the past, the great community of recorded human experience." To represent this community and its individual members with accuracy, insight, and compassion is the primary obligation Stegner places on fiction. And because these human circumstances are endlessly varied, Stegner always kept the classroom open to a wide range of representational strategies. "He did not pontificate or indoctrinate," Wendell Berry recalls in one of his essays, adding that for Stegner, the "emphasis was on workmanship," with "no specific recipe or best way." This non-dogmatic tone has continued as the hallmark of the fiction workshops, and Scowcroft catches it nicely when he explains, "We weren't trying to create a particular school of writers. We upheld a certain standard. You didn't have to write a certain kind of fiction but you had to be serious and not shoddy, and we'd try to judge the work on its own intentions." L'Heureux, too, emphasizes the program's twin commitment to openness and craft in his preface to this catalog. His pride in the seminar's success at fostering both skill and diversity is also echoed in many of the fiction writers' personal memories of their time at Stanford. Al Young and Scott Turow are especially informative as they recall the firm but generous insistence on the basics of good writing, while Tillie Olsen beautifully recaptures the intellectual ferment of the workshop's "comradeship of books and writing human beings."

Stegner's counterpart in poetry was Yvor Winters, who had been on the Stanford faculty since 1928. Critic as well as poet, Winters was already a major figure in American letters when Stegner founded the Creative Writing Program in 1946. And in the years immediately afterwards, he consolidated this reputation, first with the publication of *In Defense of Reason* (1947), the definitive statement of his critical principles, and then with his *Collected Poems* (1952). A forceful personality with sharply defined views, Winters insisted that poetry's goal is truth and its medium the rational imagination. From these premises, he developed a highly formalist, militantly anti-Romantic position that made him harshly critical not only of most modernist verse but also of many classic, canonical poets.

Winters was also a passionate teacher, and since the early 1930s he had regularly gathered about him a small but devoted group of student poets. The Creative Writing Program enabled him to formalize, in effect, this practice of nearly two decades, and until his retirement in 1966 he organized the poetry workshops around a few carefully selected young writers who could benefit from the vigor of his mind. Winters's impact on these apprentice poets was enormous. Sometimes there was a conjunction of temperaments that produced the happy communion of mentor and disciple. In most cases, there was friction, which could push students by degrees from stubborn resistance to open conflict. And occasionally there was pedagogical impasse, when Winters's aesthetic principles precluded any common ground. The poets represented here range across the entire spectrum of these possibilities. Speaking with deep affection and remarkable candor, they paint a fascinating portrait of Winters's love of poetry, his intimidating intellect, and his extraordinary humanity. Robert Pinsky records the mixture of awe, anger, and reverence that Winters evoked when he comments, "Winters was a tyrant," but two sentences later continues, "Anyway, he was a great teacher: inspiring, powerful, utterly serious, a model of intellectual integrity and passion."

In the years since Winters's retirement and his death in 1968, the influence of his ideas on the poetry workshops has continued. Kenneth Fields, one of Winters's outstanding students in the 1960s, has been a faculty member in the Creative Writing Program since 1967, and Winters's widow, poet and novelist Janet Lewis, has also led the poetry seminars from time to time. But very different voices have been introduced as well. During the decade 1968-78, the British poet Donald Davie had a major hand in conducting the poetry track, and today W. S. Di Piero and Denise Levertov extend further the range of approaches represented in the program.

The important legacy of this history is, of course, the work itself—the novels, short stories, and poems nurtured into being by classroom interaction. The twenty writers treated here are representative of the larger community of authors whose literary careers have been enlivened by the seminars. The achievements of this larger group are more fully measured by John L'Heureux's *The Uncommon Touch: Fiction and Poetry from the Stanford Writing Workshop* (1989), an anthology that includes nearly one hundred selections. All these writers have benefited from Wallace Stegner's originating vision. But Stanford in turn is no less indebted to them, since from their individual successes has grown the tradition of fine literature which makes the University's Creative Writing Program an important cultural asset. Both sides of this partnership are celebrated here.

William McPheron

Curator of British and American Literature

First Drafts, **Last Drafts**

Wendell Berry

Wendell Berry was born in 1934 and grew up in Henry County, Kentucky, where his family has lived and worked for seven generations. The first substantial period of time that he spent away from his native state began in 1958 when he accepted a Stegner Fellowship in fiction. After completing the fellowship, he remained at Stanford a second year as a Jones Lecturer in creative writing and spent another year in Europe on a Guggenheim Fellowship before moving to Manhattan to teach at New York University. Then, in 1964, Berry abandoned the literary and academic circles of New York to return to the Kentucky River valley where he had been raised. Berry's move back was not, however, an escape from the problems of industrial, urban America or from the turbulent politics and aesthetics of the 1960s. Rather, in Berry's words, he returned to "the place I was fated by birth to know better than any other" because he realized that "the world would always be most fully and clearly present" to him when perceived in the light of his own rural heritage. For the last twenty-five years, he has lived in a century-old house on a farm near Port Royal, where he cultivates 125 acres, raises sheep and draft horses, and continues to write fiction, poetry, and essays empowered by his sense of local tradition and his commitment to the land.

Berry's life as a small farmer makes him acutely aware not only of modern industry's threats to the ecology but also of the economic erosion of independent agriculture in America. With the lives and land of his own community at stake, Berry has decided to confront these issues head on. "Now that I am both native and citizen," he says, "there is no immunity to what is wrong. It is impossible to escape the sense that I am involved in history." Determined to defend his community against the recklessness of business and government, Berry addresses a variety of social problems in his essays, many of which were gathered in *Recollected Essays 1965-1980* (1981). Their subjects range from the excesses of military spending through the declining quality of education to the growing risks of nuclear power. But underlying this variety is a single purpose: all his essays, Berry explains in his most recent collection, *Home Economics* (1987), represent an "effort to describe responsibility." While written in a powerful, lucid prose, their greatest strength lies in the emotional urgency that springs from Berry's deeply rooted feelings for Port Royal. "When I have thought of the welfare of the earth," says Berry, "the problems of its health and preservation, the care of its life, I have had this place before me, the part representing the whole more vividly and accurately, making clearer and more impressing demands, than any *idea* of the whole."

Berry's attachment to Port Royal includes a strong interest in its history and social arrangements. These he explores in his novels and stories, drawing on his thorough knowledge of small-town life to create the fictional world of Port William, Kentucky. It centers around several families, tracing their lives over a period of more than a hundred years and revealing the complex responsibilities that both sustain and complicate life in the county. *Nathan Coulter* (1958), Berry's first novel, introduces us to this community, which he calls "the Port William Membership." The book's title figure is a young man coming of age in the shadows of his hard-working father, Jarrat, and his easygoing uncle, Burley. In the lives of these two older men, Nathan sees two extremes of commitment. While Jarrat works to secure title over his land, his brother Burley forgoes ownership in exchange for personal freedom that sometimes verges on recklessness. But ironically, Jarrat's obsessive desire for a homestead isolates him emotionally from his own son, and only Burley can provide Nathan the affection and respect he needs.

Since *Nathan Coulter* Berry has written three other Kentucky-based novels, including the recent *Remembering* (1988), and a collection of short stories, *The Wild Birds* (1986). This volume features six Port William stories spanning thirty-seven years.

In the title story, Burley Coulter, now seventy years old, visits his lawyer, Wheeler Catlett, to make out his will. In the testament, Burley leaves his share of the Coulter land not to his nephew, Nathan, but to Danny Branch, his illegitimate son. Wheeler objects, arguing that the land belongs to a proper member of the Coulter family. But Burley insists that a family is defined by emotional commitments, not legalities. "If he's my boy," says Burley, "I've got to treat him like he is." And he continues, "the way we are, we are members of each other. All of us. Everything. The difference ain't in who is a member and who is not, but in who knows it and who don't." For Burley, and for Berry as well, an acceptance of responsibility is the only way we can achieve our place in a community.

Berry's feelings for Kentucky also influence his reading and writing of poetry. "I am endlessly in need of the work of poets who have been concerned with living in place," he says, "the life of a place, long-term attention and devotion to a settled home and its natural household, and hence to the relation between imagination and language and place." Set in the context of his own household, Berry's poetry offers his most intimate examination of the theme of responsibility. His first eight books of verse, gathered into *The Collected Poems* in 1984, explore the value and fragility of close personal relations. Here Berry attends to the events that disrupt the normal course of life, straining the stability of marriages and friendships. Although he knows the pain of these trials, Berry also declares his belief in the rejuvenating powers of change, represented for him in the recurring cycles of nature. It is this religious faith in the renewing force of time's passage that Berry invokes in his most recent book, *Sabbaths* (1987). Consisting of poems written on Sundays over a period of eight years, the book focuses on the ties between a man, his family, and his friends. Berry carefully probes these connections and uncovers the sustaining virtue of individual commitments. In the verse dedicated to his wife on their twenty-fifth wedding anniversary, Berry describes the governing concern of his entire literary project: "Lives given to each other and/To time."

When I came to Stanford as a Stegner Fellow in 1958, I think I expected to pass through and leave it behind. Experience, of course, is much more fateful than that. Stanford, I see now, has been one of the hubs of my life. It is a common ground between me and many friends who have been dear, and indeed indispensable, to me.

And in 1958 I probably thought I had passed through my life up until then and left it behind, too. I was also wrong about that. I brought to Stanford a hundred pages or so of what was to be my first novel, *Nathan Coulter*. I began it in Kentucky and finished it at Stanford. And then, after some further wandering, I returned to Kentucky and wrote more about the place and people of *Nathan Coulter*. I am still living in Henry County, Kentucky, and still writing about the same subjects.

Wendell Berry

Selected Works by Wendell Berry

Fiction

Nathan Coulter. Boston: Houghton Mifflin, 1960; revised edition, Berkeley: North Point Press, 1985.
A Place on Earth. New York: Harcourt, Brace & World, 1967; revised edition, Berkeley: North Point Press, 1983.
The Memory of Old Jack. New York: Harcourt Brace Jovanovich, 1974.
The Wild Birds. Berkeley: North Point Press, 1986.
Remembering. Berkeley: North Point Press, 1988.

Poetry

The Broken Ground. New York: Harcourt, Brace & World, 1964.
Openings. New York: Harcourt, Brace & World, 1969.
Findings. Iowa City: Prairie Press, 1969.
Farming: A Hand Book. New York: Harcourt Brace Jovanovich, 1970.
The Country of Marriage. New York: Harcourt Brace Jovanovich, 1973.
Clearing. New York: Harcourt Brace Jovanovich, 1977.
A Part. Berkeley: North Point Press, 1980.
The Wheel. Berkeley: North Point Press, 1982.
Collected Poems. Berkeley: North Point Press, 1985.
Sabbaths. Berkeley: North Point Press, 1987.

Other

The Long-Legged House. New York: Harcourt, Brace & World, 1969.
The Hidden Wound. Boston: Houghton Mifflin, 1970.
The Unforeseen Wilderness, photographs by Eugene Meatyard. Lexington: University Press of Kentucky, 1971.
A Continuous Harmony. New York: Harcourt Brace Jovanovich, 1972.
The Unsettling of America. San Francisco: Sierra Club, 1977.
Recollected Essays 1965-1980. Berkeley: North Point Press, 1981.
The Gift of Good Land. Berkeley: North Point Press, 1981.
Standing by Words. Berkeley: North Point Press, 1983.
Home Economics. Berkeley: North Point Press, 1987.

Individual Interview

"Lyrical Plea to Preserve Fabric of Small Farms," with Keith Schneider. *New York Times,* 27 February 1988.

That night I dreamed of the lion again the way I used to, only this time he only had one eye and his voice was the sound of the wind through the leaves. Then I dreamed that Uncle Burly was with me watching the lion. And Uncle Burly laughed and said, "It'll be fine, Nathan, You're lucky. That's not a lion. You're just dreaming."

The sun in my eyes woke me, and I lay there for a while remembering where I was and watching the river. A school of bass were chasing minnows close to the shore, and I watched a blue kingfisher fly down into the willows on the other bank. Then I got up and ate the rest of the ham and biscuits for breakfast, and went on down the river.

It was a pretty morning. The sun was shining and the meadow larks were singing out across the bottoms. I felt a lot better than I had the night before. I was free and on the move, and it made me happier than I'd been for a long time.

When I got to the other side of the town where our river ran out into the Ohio I figured that I wasn't likely to meet anybody I knew, so I walked along the road and tried to catch a ride. And about the middle of the morning a man in a green truck stopped and picked me up.

I told him my name and he told me his. Then I got to thinking what a spot I'd be in if he asked me where I was going. So I asked him where he was going.

"Cincinnati," he said.

"That's where I'm going," I said.

We rode along beside the river, talking a little now and then about where we were from and the trucking business and so on. The Ohio was a bigger river than I was used to, and had more boats on it. I watched them move along in the current pushing

1.

1. Wendell Berry completed his first novel, Nathan Coulter, *in 1959 while a Stegner Fellow, and it was published a year later by Houghton Mifflin. The book, which Berry originally called* The Skull Tree, *tells the story of Nathan Coulter, a young man growing up on a Kentucky farm. The climax of the novel is Nathan's decision to leave home to escape the trauma of his grandfather's death and his own act of adultery. On the final pages of this early typescript, Nathan sleeps after a long day of travel, and then hitches a ride out of Kentucky on the following morning.*

Across the top of the draft's penultimate page Berry pens in a new element for the closing scene, Nathan's dream about a lion.

face seemed t hang in my eyes staring at me; and the chills went over me again.

I didn't know when I quit thinking about him and went t sleep.

That night I dreamed of the lion again, the dream I'd had when I was little, only now the lion was one-eyed and his voice was the soft sound of the wind through the leaves. After a while I dreamed that Uncle Burley was with me.

He laughed. "That's not a lion, Nathan. You're just dreaming."

2a.

222

"You tell Grandma," I said.

"Don't worry," Uncle Burley said. "I'll do it. You write her a letter when you get where you're going."

"I will."

"Have you got money?"

"Yes," I said.

He put his arm around me and hugged me. "Be careful, boy."

As I started out the door Jig came into the hall. "I'm going home, Burley. Hadn't I better?"

Uncle Burley said, "Stay with us, Jig. It's all right."

They went back into the living room then, and I heard the door close behind them. When I got to the yard gate and looked back I could see them through the window, sitting with Daddy by Grandpa's coffin, keeping their separate silences, their faces half shadow in the dim light.

That night, sleeping in a field beside the road, I dreamed of the lion again the same dream I'd had when I was little, only now the lion's voice was the sound of the wind through the grass, so soft I could hear my breathing. And then I dreamed that Uncle Burley was with me, and we watched the lion together.

"That's not a lion," Uncle Burley said. He spoke quietly, smiling. "You're dreaming, Nathan."

2b.

3.

2. Berry later wrote the final scene out by hand to refocus the novel's conclusion on the dream. In this manuscript version as well as in the typescript submitted to Houghton Mifflin, the morning passages are deleted and the novel ends with the dream itself. Berry and his editor made minor changes on the Houghton Mifflin typescript, in blue and red pencil respectively. Only at this stage did Berry shift the title of his novel from The Skull Tree *to* Nathan Coulter.

3. Twenty-five years after its first appearance in print, while North Point Press was preparing a new edition of Nathan Coulter, *Berry carefully revised the whole novel. He made many small changes throughout the work but also decided on one major alteration: he cut the final twenty-three pages of the original text, ending the story before Nathan's grandfather dies and before Nathan commits adultery and runs away. In part, Berry deleted this section to place* Nathan Coulter *more clearly within the context of the four other works of fiction he has since written about the Coulters and their community. But more critically, by deleting the novel's final pages, Berry redirects the focus of the conclusion away from narrative drama and towards the subtler, pyschological relationships of Nathan, his father, and his uncle. He explains, "The book now has an ending that is truer both to itself and to Nathan's part in the writings that have come since."*

Edgar Bowers

"My image of myself, apart, informed/By many deaths, resists me, and I stay/Almost as I have been, intact, aware,/Alive, though proud and cautious, even afraid." These lines conclude Edgar Bowers's "Autumn Shade," a masterful sequence of poems that explores the psychological barriers to a secure sense of self. The passage, with its quiet melancholy, its complex play of abstractions, and its exquisite formality, typifies the small, highly accomplished body of lyric poetry Bowers has published over the forty years of his writing life. His temperament draws him to the primary paradoxes of the human condition, and many of his poems probe conflicts between spirit and nature, time and eternity, life and death. This philosophical cast of mind recalls seventeenth-century metaphysical verse. Yvor Winters, in fact, considered Bowers "a great devotional poet" whose intellectual sensiblity and formal artifice continue the metaphysical tradition into the present. But Winters also recognized Bowers as a twentieth-century skeptic who breaks from the certainties of both Christian belief and Romantic faith. He is less concerned with the spiritual resolution of the antinomies his poetry addresses than with the psychological conflicts they dramatize. The harmony his art proposes is not the perfected order of the transcendental but the perilous balance of opposites within the immediate--its goal, in Bowers's own words, is "to find the perfect note, emotional/And mental, each the other one's reproach."

Born in 1924 in Rome, Georgia, Edgar Bowers grew up in the South. After graduating from Boys' High School in Decatur, a small town outside Atlanta, he entered the University of North Carolina. But in 1943 his studies were interrupted by the military draft, which took him to Germany, where he served in counter-intelligence until 1945. After the war Bowers spent an additional year in Europe before returning to Chapel Hill, completing his undergraduate degree in the spring of 1947. He arrived at Stanford the following September to study poetry with Winters, an experience vividly recreated in his reminiscence, "My First Encounter with Arthur Yvor Winters." Two years later Bowers submitted "Palm Sunday and Other Poems" for his master's thesis. Another year in Europe then intervened before Bowers came back to Stanford to finish his doctoral degree in English and begin an academic career that started with appointments first to the faculty of Duke University and then to Harpur College, now the State University of New York at Binghamton. Since 1958, when he was awarded a Guggenheim Fellowship, Bowers has lived in Santa Barbara and taught at the University of California there.

Bowers takes the title of his first book of poetry, *The Form of Loss* (1956), from a passage in "The Prince," one of the volume's several dramatic monologues. Spoken by a German aristocrat who has compromised his principles by failing to oppose the Nazis, the poem is occasioned by the execution of the nobleman's son, who has just been shot as a German spy. Seeing in the young man's fate a mirror of his own moral defeat, the prince remarks: "My son, who was the heir/To every hope and trust, grew out of caring/Into the form of loss as I had done,/And then betrayed me who betrayed him first." For Bowers, loss is the dominant condition of human life. Its persistence and enormity act as a powerful lure to despair, which must be countered by the courage he terms "caring." Poem after poem in *The Form of Loss* charts the tensions that generate loss in its many guises, while also quietly asserting the conditions that nurture care. The book opens and closes with moving testimonies to the conflict between artistic vision and execution, a struggle that animates Bowers's poetry and produces the poignancy at its heart. Other poems follow the model of "The Prince" and explore conflicts between intention and act, will and coercion in the political sphere, dramatizing them through such embattled figures of European history as William Tyndale and Charlemagne.

But *The Form of Loss'* s most impressive poems are those in which Bowers personalizes the pain death inflicts on the living. "Late Winter Night," "The Mountain Cemetery," and "Dark Earth and Summer" all confront this emotional trauma. While refusing the consolations of religion, each poem seeks a way to deal with the question, "What recompense, or pity, or deceit/Can cure, or what assumed serenity/ Conceal the mortal loss which we repeat?" And the task they collectively share is to avoid lapsing into that "mind of constant will," which is so corroded "with constant hurt" that it is "passionless, inert," with "no meaning and no place." Bowers proposes no easy solutions to this challenge, rejecting not only the eternity of Christian heaven and the spiritual unity of Romantic pantheism but also the permanent memorial promised by art. For Bowers, all of these traditional refuges from despair are ultimately deceits, and it is only the stubborn mind's solitary act of resistance that can truly sustain care and keep hope alive. "Who dares to take his living at no cost?," he asks and then responds, "We rather lose it all, lest patient rage/Be put aside before it, too, must end." And, perhaps, "patient rage" most accurately describes the poems in *The Form of Loss* --both the patience and the rage caught in their fierce formality, which balances Bowers's desire for order against his recognition of its impossibility.

Nearly a decade elapsed before the appearance of Bowers's second book of poetry, *The Astronomers* (1965). The title derives from the volume's opening poem, "The Astronomers of Mont Blanc," which is immediately followed by "Adam's Song to Heaven." These two poems, Winters argued in his *Forms of Discovery,* are among Bowers's very best work, continuing his uncompromising encounter with the limits of the human condition. Both measure the distance between the ideal and the real--"The Astronomers of Mont Blanc" in epistemological terms; "Adam's Song to Heaven," from the perspective of religion--and each imagines an unbridgeable chasm separating the static order of the ideal from the unstable realm of the real. But though this conflict entails loss, Bowers chooses here to foreground the remote, inhuman character of the ideal and thus implicitly to celebrate the quotidian world's "warm variety of risk." This pattern also informs *The Astronomers'* concluding sequence, "Autumn Shade," which treats the philosophical split between essence and existence in terms of the psychological conflict between the ideal intellectual self and the actual phenomenal self. Here Bowers weighs more heavily the suffering inflicted by daily life's contamination of the ideal, but the poem's final gesture is to embrace, albeit cautiously and sadly, the flawed world that is our inevitable fate.

This mixed stance of pained loss and regretful recovery is elaborated further in the small group of new poems featured at the end of Bowers's third collection, *Living Together* (1973), a volume which also reprints his previous two books. After its publication, another long silence occurred before the chapbook *Witnesses* appeared in 1981. This suite of five short soliloquies spoken by the Old Testament figures of Adam, Eve, Cain, Noah, and Jacob reasserts Bowers's remarkable mastery of the dramatic monologue. The poems not only recall his earlier personae, especially his recreation of the voices of Adam and Oedipus, but also refine the complex interplay Bowers achieves between mythic archetype, the poem's speaker, and its language. Taken in conjunction with his recent "Thirteen Views of Santa Barbara" and *For Louis Pasteur,* a new collection due from Princeton University Press later this year, *Witnesses* promises to open a new chapter in Bowers's literary career--a prospect enhanced by his receiving the prestigious Bollingen Prize in Poetry in 1989.

On the Composition of *Thirteen Views of Santa Barbara*

The desire to write a group of poems about Santa Barbara came to me at an exhibit of Hokusai's *Thirty-Six Views of Mount Fuji* at the Santa Barbara Museum of Art. Earlier, I had intended to write a short ode on the sport of hang-gliding as seen from La Cumbre Peak, the highest elevation behind Santa Barbara; and I began the group with a poem ostensibly about hang-gliding and including some of the elements that might have gone into the ode but which became, instead, topics recurrent in the group, topics historical and moral by which the group would be developed.

Each poem—except for numbers one and thirteen, which are meant to be a frame and commentary for the group, and numbers six and nine, which refer to persons I have known—is a reflection on places in Santa Barbara or its vicinity that I have often visited and for which pictures of another kind might be provided and for which I have provided a few. The first poem might be illustrated by several views, some of the city and its location between the mountains and the sea, as seen, first, from La Cumbre Peak and then following the imagined flight of the hang-glider; then by persons, places, and objects that recall the history of the place; and, finally, by my own memory of a more recent history but with the same moral context, ending in an American cemetery in England, where many "hang-gliders" are buried or named, a cemetery for which other pictures might be provided. For the exhibit, I have provided amateurish photographs of a few of the sites as I might have recalled each while writing the poem with its name. It would be possible, of course, to provide an album of such photographs, not only of the sites named in the titles, but also of particulars and moments of the Santa Barbara world referred to in the group as a whole.

To the original thirteen poems I later added one about the Vedanta Temple, as a little saga of the American Protestant experience, and an "epilogue" entitled "The Yacht" (the only poem not written in blank verse), which is an imitation of a sonnet by Hérédia, itself an imitation of Classical poems, in order to contrast a Classical purity, simplicity, and distance of feeling to the complex and personal feeling of the group as a whole.

In further imitation of Hokusai, I could write as many miscellaneous poems as I please, so long as each is set in Santa Barbara or refers to its places or people; but the group is united by topics present from the beginning about which enough seems to be said, at least for the time being and with the Santa Barbara setting. I was to develop them further in poems about other subjects.

And again like Hokusai, though I added two poems, I retained the original title, which, of course, suggests Wallace Stevens' "Thirteen Ways of Looking at a Blackbird," and which invites, I hope not too seriously, a comparison with his poem.

The original thirteen first appeared in the Summer 1987 issue of *The Threepenny Review*. The final fifteen are to be the contents of a chapbook from Occasional Works and will be in *For Louis Pasteur*, to be published by the Princeton University Press in 1989.

Edgar Bowers

Selected Works by Edgar Bowers

Poetry

The Form of Loss. Denver: Swallow, 1956.
The Astronomers. Denver: Swallow, 1965.
Living Together: New and Selected Poems. Boston: Godine, 1973.
Witnesses. Los Angeles: Symposium Press, 1981.

Much of the imagery in Edgar Bowers's "Thirteen Views of Santa Barbara" derives from actual scenes in and about the California city where the poet has lived since 1958. For the occasion of this exhibit, Bowers took snapshots of many of these settings, including the sites for "The Botanic Gardens," where "Poppies bloom in the meadow below the mountain," and "The Museum of Natural History," at whose entrance, "leviathan awaits/Exodus to the promised deeper sea." About these photographs and their relation to the poems, Bowers comments: "The few pictures one might exhibit would be illustrations, as it were, of what might be done more completely if, say, there were a volume of poem and picture—pictures taken, I should hope, by a photographer more professional than I! though I think the amateurish and 'personal' quality of the ones I provide might give a dimension to my acquaintance with the sites more nearly true to the way I thought of the sites; whereas the more professional product might make it seem that I was writing poems about pictures!"

"The Court House" is the twelfth poem in Bowers's "Thirteen Views of Santa Barbara." Its relation to the scene of its title is typical of the sequence as a whole. At the poem's foundation is a precise but artful description of the court house, a compositional process that can be analyzed through Bowers's photographs. His exterior shot is the visual counterpart of the poem's account of the building's "Moorish-Latin" architecture, while the interior shot offers a standard by which to measure Bowers's treatment of the murals picturing the Spanish soldier Juan Cabrillo

and the Franciscan priest Junípero Serra. Bowers's verbal rendition of these paintings merges imperceptibly into an imaginative vision of the whole of Santa Barbara County, which terminates at one end in the wells extracting "imperial oil" and at the other in the "dry fields/For blast-off" at Vandenberg Air Force Base. This panoramic view of the region is reflected in the photograph Bowers took from the top of the court house. All this

physical description serves the poem's thematic focus on the nature of political ambition and empire. Bowers introduces the theme in his opening stanza by mentioning Napoleon's tomb, an allusion that directs attention to the ideology of the court house's decorative style as well as to other signs of economic and cultural imperialism that are visible on the Santa Barbara landscape.

Thirteen Views of Santa Barbara

The Court House

On the walls around Napoleon are depicted
His true remains. These studied images,
Civic narrations and expectancies,
Move those who go to wonder at his tomb
Like shapes that move through water as a wave.

Our Moorish-Latin court house! Murals bring
Cabrillo shoreward. Junipero Serra's flock
Watch blind desire apportion earth and sea
On scales of gold. Green tree and kingly ranch
Spread from imperial oil to the western gate:

Acres of flowers for seed; nearby, dry fields
For blast-off, for failure and failed ambition
Past intimate horizon to the far.
We who had sought the spirit's inbetween
To have life more abundantly, discoverers

From inbetween's anxiety, explore
The court rooms, like a logic, for a premise,
Uneasy before the flags and photographs
Of boys who traveled east to fight a war
With other boys equally free and brave.

Raymond Carver

When Raymond Carver died in August 1988, contemporary letters lost a uniquely arresting and compassionate voice. With his first major collection of stories, *Will You Please Be Quiet, Please?* (1976), Carver opened new territories to fiction's exploration of the American psyche. Drawing characters from his personal world of the hard-working poor, he uses a language of precise detail to invoke the repressed violence, thwarted desires, and terrifying emptiness lying just below the surface of everyday lives. Carver's disquieting but sympathetic vision of ordinary people at the breaking point intensifies in his next book, *What We Talk about When We Talk about Love* (1981), which consolidated his reputation as a master of the short story. Though critical acclaim was quick and emphatic in the decade after 1976, Carver's success had not come easily. It was won from a long and difficult apprenticeship to both his art and his life.

Born in 1938 into a blue-collar family that migrated to the West during the Great Depression, Carver grew up in Yakima, Washington. His father worked as a filer at the local sawmill and mesmerized his son by telling family tales and reading aloud from Zane Grey westerns. With a dreary future in the mill before him, Carver dreamed of becoming a writer. While still a teenager, he translated his love for fishing and hunting into stories and took a mail order course in creative writing. But just after graduation in 1957, Carver married his high school sweetheart, started at the mill, and soon became the father of two children. Thus began twenty "ferocious years of parenting"—decades of "unrelieved responsibilty and permanent distraction," as Carver later described them. But if his youth was lost, his dream of writing was not. Carver moved the family to California in 1958 and enrolled in Chico State College, working a series of menial jobs at night. Here his commitment to serious writing was galvanized by the young novelist John Gardner, whose creative writing course and individual attention proved decisive. "A writer's values and craft. This is what the man taught and what he stood for," Carver explained, "and this is what I've kept by me in the years since that brief but all-important time."

Battling endless "crap jobs" and each day's "wagonload of frustration," Carver persisted, eventually completing his undergraduate degree at Humboldt State College in 1963 and spending a year at the University of Iowa's Writers Workshop before returning to California. In 1967 he moved into his first white-collar job as a textbook editor at a Palo Alto firm. There followed a National Endowment for the Arts fellowship, Carver's first academic appointments, and, in 1972-73, a Stegner Fellowship at Stanford. But as his professional circumstances improved, what Carver called the "spiritual obliteration" of his daily life accelerated. During the same years he developed the distinctive style of his stories, Carver began drinking seriously, a condition that worsened through the mid-1970s.

In his essay "Fires," Carver recounts this harrowing period, when he learned that "I had to bend or else break. And I also learned that it is possible to bend and break at the same time." The desperation and confinement of those years govern the stories in Carver's first two collections. Bleakly bearing witness to the people of the underclass, with whom Carver felt his deepest kinship, they employ familiar settings and matter-of-fact language but everywhere suggest the powerful undercurrents of emotion that disrupt and shatter normalcy. "So Much Water So Close to Home," a story first published in 1975 and later revised for *What We Talk about When We Talk about Love,* probes the trauma caused by a husband's callous handling of the naked corpse of a young girl that he and his fishing buddies find during an outing in the mountains. As the wife struggles to comprehend her husband's behavior, she recognizes in the victim's nude body an image of the psychological isolation and sexual violence that threaten her marriage. As thoughts of the murdered girl infiltrate the most incidental elements of her life, she feels more and more distant from her husband, and a vague sense of fear settles over the household. Carver's artistry renders this situation so intensely that readers are overwhelmed by its hopelessness. We watch the characters bend under unrelenting pressure and painfully realize that if change ever comes, it will be at the cost of breaking.

During 1977 a different but equally dramatic change came to Carver himself. In June, after several hospitalizations in the preceding months, Carver quit drinking. That year also marked the end of his twenty-year marriage—followed shortly by Carver's meeting the critically acclaimed poet Tess Gallagher at a writers' conference and establishing with her a relationship that stabilized and sustained him for the rest of his life. This recovery and renewal profoundly affected Carver's writing. In 1983, when he compiled *Fires,* a retrospective collection of essays, poems, and stories, "So Much Water So Close to Home" appeared in a substantially different form. For this version Carver returned to the text of the story as it was originally printed prior to inclusion in *What We Talk about When We Talk about Love.* Here the dialogue between the characters is more open, their conversations suggesting a dynamic of mutual caring. Though frustration and menace still persist, the story does not capitulate to their power. Rather, it shows how charity can erode the barriers separating men and women.

This more generous interpretation of human character deepens in *Cathedral,* the new story collection Carver wrote with a rush of creative energy in just over eighteen months and published the same year as *Fires.* The volume's title story had, in fact, been the first sign of Carver's greater optimism. "Cathedral," he explained in an interview, "was very much an 'opening up' process for me." It "*was* a larger, grander story than anything I had previously written" and, he added, "it reflects a change in my life as much as it does in my way of writing." The story begins in barely suppressed conflict. A husband is angry at a visit from a blind man, whose close friendship with his wife dates from years before the couple met. Through most of the evening irritation simmers until, late at night, with the two sitting alone before a television program on cathedrals, the blind man asks the husband to describe one. The husband takes his hand, and together they trace a picture of a cathedral. For the husband this moment of human connection "was like nothing else in my life up to now."

Carver continued to explore the aesthetic implications of this affirmative vision in *Where I'm Calling From.* Appearing just three months before his death in 1988, it features not only new stories but also selections from each of his major collections since *Will You Please Be Quiet, Please.* Perhaps the book's most moving story—and certainly its most surprising—is the concluding piece, "Errand," which won first prize in the 1988 O. Henry Short Story Awards. Here Carver turned away from contemporary America to focus on the death of Chekhov. Though the subject is a commonplace of literary history, Carver casts the event into the idiom of everyday life and endows the factual record with astonishing mystery and poignancy. A profound meditation on the inconsequentiality of death as well as an homage to Chekhov, "Errand" shows Carver still boldly testing the limits of himself and his art.

I don't think there should be any barriers, artificial or otherwise, between life as it's lived and life as it's written about.

Imagination and Autobiography
The stories and poems I've written are not autobiographical, but there is a starting point in the real world for everything I've written. Stories just don't come out of thin air; they come from someplace, a wedding of imagination and reality, a little autobiography and a lot of imagination.

To write a novel, it seemed to me, a writer should be living in a world that makes sense, a world that the writer can believe in, draw a bead on, and then write about accurately. A world that will, for a time anyway, stay fixed in one place. Along with this there has to be a belief in the essential *correctness* of that world. A belief that the known world has reasons for existing, and is worth writing about, is not likely to go up in smoke in the process. This wasn't the case with the world I knew and was living in. My world was one that seemed to change gears and directions, along with its rules, every day.

On Writing and Revision
I try to write the story as quickly as I can. I don't think I've ever written more than two or three stories where it's taken more than two days to write the first draft. Usually I just plunge on, even though I don't always know what I'm doing, and try to get something out on the page.

In one regard I was in no hurry to finish the story or the poem I was working on, for finishing something meant I'd have to find the time, and the belief, to begin something else. So I had great patience with a piece of work after I'd done the initial writing...changing this, adding that, cutting out something else.

Language and the Origins of the Story
When I'm writing I don't think in terms of developing symbols or of what an image will do.... They seem to evolve, occur. I truly invent them and *then* certain things seem to form around them as events occur, recollection and imagination begin to color them and so forth.

I literally start with a sentence or a line. I always have to have that first line in my head, whether it's a poem or a story. Later on everything else is subject to change, but that first line rarely changes.

Detail in Fiction
What creates tension in a piece of fiction is partly the way the concrete words are linked together to make up the visible action of the story. But it's also the things that are left out, that are implied, the landscape just under the smooth (but sometimes broken and unsettled) surface of things.

I like it when there is some feeling of threat or sense of menace in short stories.... It's possible, in a poem or a short story, to write about commonplace things and objects using commonplace but precise language, and to endow those things—a chair, a window curtain, a fork, a stone, a woman's earring—with immense, even startling power.

For the details to be concrete and convey meaning, the language must be accurate and precisely given. The words can be so precise they may even sound flat, but they can still carry; if used right, they can hit all the notes.

Raymond Carver

This collage of quotations from Alive and Writing, At the Field's End, Fires, *and* Matters of Life and Death *was suggested by Raymond Carver to serve as his statement for the exhibit.*

Selected Works by Raymond Carver

Fiction

Will You Please Be Quiet, Please?. New York: McGraw Hill, 1976.
Furious Seasons and Other Stories. Santa Barbara: Capra Press, 1977.
What We Talk about When We Talk about Love. New York: Knopf, 1981.
Cathedral. New York: Knopf, 1983.
Where I'm Calling From. New York: Atlantic Monthly Press, 1988.

Poetry

Near Klamath. Sacramento: Sacramento State College English Club, 1968.
Winter Insomnia. Santa Cruz: Kayak, 1970.
At Night the Salmon Move. Santa Barbara: Capra Press, 1976.
Where Water Comes Together with Other Water. New York: Random House, 1985.
Ultramarine. New York: Random House, 1986.

Other

Fires: Essays, Poems, Stories. Santa Barbara: Capra Press, 1983.

Individual Interviews

Alive and Writing: Interviews with American Authors of the 1980s, with Larry McCaffery and Sinda Gregory. Chicago: University of Illinois Press, 1987.
At the Field's End: Interviews with Twenty Pacific Northwest Writers, with Nicholas O'Connell. Seattle: Madrona Publishers, 1987.
"Matters of Life and Death: An Interview with Raymond Carver," with William A. Stull. *Bloomsbury Review,* January/February 1988.

1.

1. It is not surprising that Raymond Carver chose the death of Anton Chekhov to be the subject of his first historical story, collected in Where I'm Calling From (1988). He had always felt a special artistic affinity with this Russian master of the short story. "Chekhov was writing about a submerged population a hundred years ago," Carver explained. "He found a means of letting those people have their say. So in writing about people who aren't so articulate and who are confused and scared, I'm not doing anything radically different."
  The initial manuscript of "Errand," which carries the working title "Chekov," begins with assurance. Deletions and marginal notes are largely absent, suggesting the quick movement of Carver's imagination. This is typical of his practice. "It doesn't take that long to do the first draft of the story, that usually happens in one sitting," Carver said, and added, it is "most often done in longhand, I simply fill up the pages as rapidly as I can."

2. In this second draft, Carver has exactly transcribed his initial manuscript into typescript before beginning to revise by hand. "There's not much that I like better than to take a story that I've had around the house for a while and work it over again," Carver commented, "I've done as many as twenty or thirty drafts of a story, never less than ten or twelve drafts." Here Carver introduces a new title, "Room Service." Later he will change it to "Champagne," and then again to "The Mortician," before finally adopting Tess Gallagher's suggestion and calling it "Errand."

While Carver's line-by-line editing is intricate, the most important change introduced in the second draft is signalled by the arrow in the left-hand margin at the end of the second paragraph. The arrow points to an extensive passage in longhand on the back of this page, where Carver sketches the ideas and language for several new paragraphs.

3. Carver develops this new material from a single image that seems to break suddenly into his thought. Beginning in midsentence, he writes: "was doing something with his napkin when blood began gushing out of his mouth." From this point Carver unfolds the scene of Chekhov and his childhood friend, Alexei Suvorin, dining at an expensive Moscow restaurant. "Chekov was agonizingly embarrassed," and the manuscript continues: "Back at his hotel he persists in denying the gravity of the disease." In this moment Carver captures the defiance that will sustain Chekhov through seven years of chronic tuberculosis. Ironically, Carver completed this story just before he began his own battle with lung cancer.

4. As Carver's imagination developed the scene in the Moscow restaurant, it became so emotionally charged that he made it the opening of the story. After numerous drafts of intensive line-by-line revision, Carver then sought Tess Gallagher's editorial advice. The handwriting on this draft is predominantly hers and shows her proposal of a new title, "Errand." On the final page of an even later draft, Gallagher reworks in manuscript the concluding lines, which Carver then revises in his own hand. But even at this stage, the story is far from complete. Before publication Carver continued to elaborate the details of individual scenes to quicken the narrative flow.

2.

3.

4.

Evan S. Connell

When Evan S. Connell arrived at Stanford in the fall of 1947 to attend classes for a year in the newly established Creative Writing Program, he was already committed to a writing career. Connell had reached that decision before he was twenty-one, while serving as an aviation cadet in the United States Navy during the Second World War. After his discharge, he took a degree in English at the University of Kansas, where he began the formal study of fiction that he continued at Stanford under Wallace Stegner and that year's visiting professor, Katherine Anne Porter.

Connell began by concentrating on the short story. A piece he wrote during his stay at Stanford, "I'll Take You to Tennessee," not only won the University's Edith Mirrielees Short Story Award in 1948 but also was selected for the 1949 volume of O. Henry Prize Stories. Connell's first book, *The Anatomy Lesson and Other Stories* (1957), collected these early works and clearly declared his mastery of the form--no fewer than four of the volume's pieces had already been featured in either *Prize Stories* or *Best American Short Stories*.

In the three decades since this remarkable beginning, Connell has explored a variety of prose forms, both extending the boundaries of conventional fiction and opening new territories for nonfiction. "Every story," Connell says, demands "a different style," and he himself has relentlessly searched out the most evocative forms for the many different stories he has told over the years.

From the late 1950s through the mid-1970s, Connell directed his creative energy into novels. Of the six he published during this period, *Mrs. Bridge* (1959) and its companion volume, *Mr. Bridge* (1969), are emblematic of his achievement. Set in the Kansas City social world that Connell knew as a youth, these complementary books record the hauntingly empty lives of an upper-middle-class couple. *Mrs. Bridge* portrays a woman accomplished in the proprieties of privilege but sadly helpless before the emotional isolation that attends her wealth. *Mr. Bridge* transposes this emptiness into a masculine key, tracing the class prejudices that drain joy from both worldly success and domestic comfort. Refracting many of the same events through the separate personalities of wife and husband, the novels project a complex, compelling image of Midwestern bourgeois life.

Connell's achievement inevitably recalls Sinclair Lewis's classic depictions of provincial middle-class culture in the 1920s. But this comparison underscores Connell's distinctiveness, for his art possesses a psychological intimacy that pushes social satire into more deeply human dimensions of irony. Connell accomplishes this by fracturing the narrative lines of both his novels into more than a hundred separately-titled vignettes. These brief sections, each precisely registering a single moment in the character's life, respect the conventions of traditional realism—but they also reach beyond them. Like pieces of shattered mirrors, they fragment their subjects, distracting readers from plot and narrowing concentration to the most telling details of the characters' personal lives.

This play of tradition and innovation is a signature of Connell's practice and is conspicuously imprinted on two experimental works that he wrote parallel to the novels. *Notes from a Bottle Found on the Beach at Carmel* (1963) and *Points for a Compass Rose* (1973) draw facts, stories, and quotations from Connell's extensive reading of history and interweave these pieces of the human past into sequences that defy formal categorization. Critics most often classify them as poetry, but they have also been treated as fiction and as epic. Connell himself proposes no particular label, commenting instead, "I was putting everything into the books I thought appropriate. I wanted to make them as complex as possible. I like things that can't be solved." The volumes are, perhaps, best read as the efforts of a contemporary mind to situate itself amid the contradictory plenitude of anthropological, historical, scientific, and philosophic data that permeate our culture. "Arbitrarily," Connell observes midway through *Notes from a Bottle*, "we circumscribe reality, choosing to limit/the universe to the bounds of our apprehension," but we also perversely insist that our fabrications are true, our boundaries absolute. Meditating on the long record of folly, violence, and despair that springs from this confusion, Connell refuses to posit yet another totalizing fiction. Rather, these innovative books plunge the reader directly into the shock of our collective heritage, inducing powerful feelings of unease and skepticism. "You aren't supposed to understand it," Connell explains; his goal is to evoke the "limitless depth" of perception that confounds intellectual certainty.

Connell continues to transform traditional literary conventions by infusing them with new methods and fresh subjects, but in the last ten years he has shifted the arena to nonfiction. He recently remarked that "I read a lot of nonfiction: archeological, anthropological, historical. The overtones are often so much greater than in fiction." Certainly these overtones distinguish the essays in *A Long Desire* (1979) and *The White Lantern* (1980). The books are linked by a common concern with powerful obsessions and their uncanny grip on human behavior. *A Long Desire* treats explorers and travelers, focusing particularly on "the singular person, inexplicably drawn from familiar comforts toward a nebulous goal, lured often enough to death—it is he, or she, whose peregrinations can never be thoroughly understood." *The White Lantern* revolves around quests more intellectual than geographical, including discoveries in both the natural and the social sciences. When in an early chapter Connell describes an Italian peasant crashing through the roof of an Etruscan burial vault to find himself suddenly surrounded by the artifacts of a wholly alien culture, we immediately recognize an image of our own amazed experience of the book, for it, too, thrusts us into worlds of fact that are at once close at hand and deeply strange.

Connell's success in animating such documentary material springs in part from his mastery of the resonant detail. He has a singular ability to seize eccentric, often mundane, but always revealing bits of information that cast unexpected shadows across otherwise familiar scenes. Under the spell of his prose, events miraculously escape the generalizations we use to imprison and domesticate them, boldly reclaiming their essential mystery. Nowhere is this process more evident than in Connell's latest work of nonfiction, *Son of the Morning Star* (1984). Though this book about General George Armstrong Custer and the battle at the Little Bighorn is intensely researched, it is no traditional exercise in biography or popular history. With startling details enlivening his narrative innovations, Connell transforms both these genres into a unique work that is "as unconventional and daring as was its main protagonist." So wrote Paul Andrew Hutton, reviewer for *Western American Literature,* who continued, "*Son of the Morning Star* restores Custer to his proper place in history as a brave, experienced, and driven soldier full of compelling contradictions, and hopefully dismantles forever the cardboard buffoon of recent popular culture."

Q: *Could you describe the history of your interest in Custer?*
A: My earliest recollection of Custer is a portrait of him, and one of Sitting Bull, that I got for sending in some cereal box-tops--Quaker Oats, I think--when I was ten or twelve years old. Beyond that, he was only a part of my interest in frontier history. Wyatt Earp, Billy the Kid, *et al.* were giants in those days. Later I visited quite a few Western historical sites, including the Little Bighorn field, and still later, when I was planning a book of essays about the old West, it seemed obvious that Custer should be included. Then I got so absorbed in reading about the debacle that I gave up my original idea and devoted the book almost entirely to him.

Q: *How did your understanding and judgment of Custer and Sitting Bull change as your research progressed and you began to write?*
A: My opinion of Custer didn't change much during the research. I had always thought of him as impetuous and brave, perhaps not as cautious as he should have been, but after reading so much about him my understanding naturally increased. I had known very little about his family life and early career. As for Sitting Bull, I knew even less--which is to say, absolutely nothing except that he had been the opposing figurehead.

Q: *Your use of details throughout* Son of the Morning Star *is especially striking. Do you think that as a fiction writer your selection of details is fundamentally different from the typical historian's? Could you give an example?*
A: The book differs from most Custer books in that I was fascinated by details irrelevant to the campaign. For instance: Gall enjoyed listening to Mendelssohn's "Wedding March." Satanta committed suicide by diving head first from a second-floor window of a prison hospital. Lieutenant Calhoun actually carried a cake into the great fight, intending to celebrate the Seventh Cavalry triumph. I could not resist including such trivia, which considerably lengthened the book and exasperated proper scholars, who felt that I should have stuck to military essentials. So many bizarre and touching examples of humanity turned up that a proposed essay of some twenty pages expanded to more than 700.

Q: *Why did you end the book with the story of Kate Bighead?*
A: I knew Kate Bighead should end the story as soon as I read about her telling Dr. Marquis that her pony might have kicked dirt on Custer's body. I never questioned this immediate, intuitive decision. It felt right, so I didn't bother to explain it to myself logically. A year or so after reading the Marquis account I came upon Charles Kuhlman's 1951 book, which also concluded with the Cheyenne woman, and was dismayed. He had stolen my ending. But then, after many long and private debates, I resolved to use it anyway. Custer scholars would accuse me of plagiarizing his idea, I thought, even though I hadn't. If I had read Kuhlman before Marquis, the book might have ended differently--or maybe not.

Q: *Did the photographs, particularly the portraits, affect your perception of the figures and events? What role do you see them playing for the reader?*
A: Photographs had little influence, if any. I was interested, and sometimes mildly surprised, by the appearance of one man or another, but that didn't affect the narrative. The North Point editors were mildly in favor of including photos. I was mildly opposed because this wasn't meant to be an academic documentary so much as an impression or interpretation, and I thought photos could be distracting. Harper & Row wanted to use photos in the paperback, and I didn't object. Some readers need them, others don't.

Q: *Your work of the past decade seems to depart from fiction. How much of a departure is it, in fact? What aspects of history, natural history, and the sciences have drawn you away from the traditional novel?*

A: For the past decade I've written very little fiction, but this isn't a conscious departure—it's just that a variety of historical subjects interested me and I wanted to explore them. I might return to fiction. At present I am working on "The Alchymist's Journal"—the meditations of seven quasi-fictional figures. I do think non-fiction is easier because so little imagination is required; it seems to consist mostly of research, selection, organization, and presentation. All of this can be tedious, but seems less difficult than the attempt to make imaginary beings credible.

Q: *Has researching and presenting factual material affected your style? Do you feel there are major stylistic differences between* Son of the Morning Star *and your novels?*

A: The time spent these past several years on factual material has perhaps reminded me of the need for lucidity and for concision. As to narrative style, I've always tried to employ whatever style or approach seemed effective, whether fiction or nonfiction. There could be stylistic differences between the novels and the historical essays, but I've never thought about it and don't see much significance in the idea.

Q: *Is there another historical figure you would consider writing on with the same depth as Custer?*

A: I have no immediate plans for a book similar to Custer, but it's possible. Any number of wild men ranged the western frontier, and the world, and I never grow tired of hearing about them, but for now I have little in mind except finishing the alchymy book.

Q: Son of the Morning Star *has received extraordinary reviews. What pleased you the most about reviewers' comments? Were there aspects of the book's reception that you did not like, or felt missed some of the book's value?*

A: One always anticipates superb reviews and can't help feeling peeved by the ignorance and/or stupidity of reviewers who did not think the book quite that great. Some of the Custer reviews were hostile, three or four quite slashing and sneering. I halfway expected this, if for no other reason than that Custer's name invariably starts a squabble—which is noteworthy. I can think of no other American figure who arouses such passion, possibly excepting Sherman in the South.

The only reviews that surprised me were those that found the work dull. I thought it might be faulted for various reasons—eccentric structure, levity, interpretation, military analysis—but I was myself so absorbed by the subject that I could hardly imagine anybody finding it dull. The research and writing took well over three years, seven days a week, with very few intermissions. I visited the battlefield five times and scoured forty or fifty libraries. Once I decided to take a vacation, so I flew to Cancun for a week, and sat on the beach counting down the days until I could get back to work. I still have trouble with anybody who considers it a dull book, but there have been some. I'm pleased most of all to hear from those who read it more than once.

Evan S. Connell
Interview, June 1988

Selected Works by Evan S. Connell

Fiction

The Anatomy Lesson and Other Stories. New York: Viking, 1957.
Mrs. Bridge. New York: Viking, 1958.
The Patriot. New York: Viking, 1960.
At the Crossroads: Stories. New York: Simon and Schuster, 1965.
The Diary of a Rapist. New York: Simon and Schuster, 1966.
Mr. Bridge. New York: Knopf, 1969.
The Connoisseur. New York: Knopf, 1974.
Double Honeymoon. New York: Putnam, 1976.
St. Augustine's Pigeon: The Selected Stories. Berkeley: North Point Press, 1980.

Poetry

Notes from a Bottle Found on the Beach at Carmel. New York: Viking, 1963.
Points for a Compass Rose. New York: Knopf, 1973.

Other

A Long Desire. New York: Holt, Rinehart and Winston, 1979.
The White Lantern. New York: Holt, Rinehart and Winston, 1980.
Son of the Morning Star: Custer and the Little Bighorn. Berkeley: North Point Press, 1985.

Individual Interview

Fiction!: Interviews with Northern California Novelists, with Dan Tooker and Roger Hofheins. New York: Harcourt Brace Jovanovich, 1976.

1.

look for C's discussions   Chivington p. 294, 143
crippled officers p. 10 Da   Rottenbelly 278
W.L. buffalo calf 10
Araphaoe spies 204 W.
Dull Knife other names 205 W.L.   "White Horse" II°L, Devil's Lake 1871-91
"Major Reno had a half-a-gallon keg that he took with him in the
field, but I don't believe any other officer emptied its contents."
(Myth 149/Godfrey's Narrative) Custer "absolutely abstemious"
Gibbon 450/Terry 1000
Benteen: at my own request Terry permitted me to mount what was left
of my troop and go to C's field soon after he joined us on 27th
Myth 229: Reno: "The Indians are the best light cavalry in the world
I have seen pretty nearly all of them, and I do except even the
Cossacks." (responding to criticisms by C's roommate, Gen T.L. Rosser
Cheyenne Charles Sitting Man "the last witness of the Custer fight"
died 1961 (Liberty 72)
Stewart 433: Since "there is no such thing as a coherent and unbiased
account of the Custer disaster..."
Stewart 212: "troop" instead of "Company" when speaking of cavalry was
officially designated in '83, although used on muster rolls at
least 2 years earlier (Troop replaced Co around 1880)
Andrist 249: "Company" still used in 76 and after, replaced by "troop"
in next decade or so.
Camp: Custer 617 men plus 53 scouts/packers
Ambrose: 611
Reno: "I had 112 officers and men and some 25 scouts" in valley (Myth
                                                                    611
Reno hill: 14 officers/359 men/14 others=367   22
"More has actually been written concerning this relatively small
and insignificant skirmish than about the great struggle at
Gettysburg, the turning point of our bloody Civil War. Daniel
Magnussen 186(?)'s Narrative)
T's: averaged 48 per company at battle time; left Lincoln with
32/714 but 126 left at Powder base camp
T's, p111: "Benteen had 5 officers, 116 men; Reno 9,127,2 doctors plus
T's 180: Knipe/despatched by Tom with verbal order from general
to pack train to hurry. K reached Benteen mile west of Lone Tree
and B sent him on back to McD
Varnum was C's chief of scouts, had 41 Rees on June 25, about 1/2
vanished but reappeared on 28th
Bradley was G's chief of scouts
Bloody Knife (tart individual, sometimes impertinent, who twitted
Custer about his marksmanship the whites and was so little impress
by Custer's marksmanship that he once told the general he couldnot
hit a tent from inside. (Ambrose 337)
Two of Porter's assistants fainted while holding chloroform-soaked
sponges. Girard took over. (Camp 256)
Crook's beard forked naturally beneath his chin and for one reason
or another -- possibly to keep from gathering so much dust in
the field -- he occasionally braided the two halves, producing an
unforgettable impression on anybody who saw him. (Andrist 249)
Sheridan retired (Ranker as Dept. of Mo. in Sept '67) Until Oct Sheridan [Div. of Mo.]
Sherman was Dept. of Mo t Hancock dept. Co in Mar '67 (Dippie 4)
Benteen's daughter dies [Mealsron 257]
Lydia Ann Kirkpatrick married David Reed in 1845. [Ludials put. / half Sisi
Libbie revised & expanded his letters   [Fotheaston '68
Norma XV, 61 buffalo hunt   Iron Mail p. 1528-1159
                             Sioux encampment [Coon 177]
                             Killed staghounds [Coon 173]

2.

The obedient sergeant commandeered two enlisted men and these guinea
pigs galloped forward while Roe and the others followed. Very soon a familiar
noise was heard: Pop! Pop! Pop! Pop!

Neither the intrepid sergeant nor his companions were hit, but the
plateau was by now carpeted with Indians and Lt. Roe thought it wise to retreat,
which he did in good order.

Various members of the army kept diaries or journals, among them

Captain Henry Freeman. Unlike most of his companions he
disciplined blue-jacketed riders on the ridge might be hostile, and
despite rumors that two of them had been seen shaking hands with Roe
he bet a cigar on it.

That night while discussing the day's events most of Terry's infantrymen
more unpleasant news, whereas the cavalrymen
-- emotionally related to Custer's 7th -- argued that if indeed there had
been a fight Custer must have been victorious. "So obstinate is human
nature," Bradley wrote, "that there were actually men in the command who
lay down to sleep that night in the firm conviction, notwithstanding all
the disclosures of the day, that there was not an Indian in our front...
They could explain ingeniously every circumstance that had a contrary look,
and to argue with them was worse than useless."

Tuesday morning there was not an Indian anywhere.
Farther up the valley a number of pale unidentifiable objects were
east of the river. They were assumed to be
dead buffalo -- several dark objects among the carcasses thought to be
buffalo skins left behind when the Indians fled. Bradley crossed
the river to investigate.

Soon after his departure the marching column reached the site of
a vast Indian encampment, so recently abandoned that the fire beds were
still warm. The earth all around was littered with debris: shotguns,

---

Early on the Sunday morning of 25 June 1876, General George Armstrong Custer led five companies of the 7th Cavalry against 3,000 Sioux and Cheyenne warriors. Two days later, the mutilated bodies of Custer's 220-man contingent were found on the banks of the Little Bighorn. Government hearings produced volumes of inconclusive testimony, numerous private memoirs added their perspectives to the controversy, and ever since, historians have fervently debated Custer's actions. Evan S. Connell's Son of the Morning Star (1984) introduces a new voice into this rich and contradictory body of literature. "More significant men of his time can be discussed without passion," Connell explains, "because they are inextricably woven into a tapestry of the past, but this hotspur refuses to die. He stands forever on that dusty Montana slope."

1. Of Son of the Morning Star Connell says, "The research and writing took well over three years, seven days a week, with very few intermissions. I visited the battlefield five times and scoured forty or fifty libraries." Connell's notes occupied hundreds of typewritten pages, each transcribing a mixture of anecdotes, dates, statistics, and fragments of eyewitness accounts. Connell carefully recorded the exact sources of this information, listing authors and page numbers of the books. These references he later gathered into Son of the Morning Star 's bibliography. As Connell integrated individual details into his narrative, he crossed through the passage, sometimes typing fresh versions of the unused portions of the research notes.

2. When Connell began shaping this huge mass of information into narrative form, rather than write successive drafts, he went "back and forth, cutting, revising, inserting," clipping paragraphs or sentences from different pages and repasting them elsewhere in the work. "I rather regretted doing it like that," Connell says, "because I thought it would be interesting to watch the progression through various stages, but the book was so large and I had so much material to incorporate that I wanted to eliminate unnecessary retyping."

CAMP: Complete Roster

Third Draft
4/27/81

Broken Hoop

~~His-es-taie~~
~~at the Little Bighorn~~

I cannot help plead to my countrymen, at every
opportunity, to cherish all that is manly and
noble in the military profession, because Peace
is enervating and no man is wise enough to foretell
when soldiers may be in demand again.

...~~General~~ William Tecumseh Sherman

The nation's hoop is broken and scattered.
...Black Elk

William H. White was a soldier in the Montana column led by
Colonel John Gibbon that marched up the Little Bighorn valley during
the summer of 1876. White reports that on Monday evening, June 26,
Gibbon's men, together with those led by General Alfred Terry, reached
the site of what is now Crow Agency and there they saw hundreds of
mounted Sioux. Some of these warriors, *challenged the soldiers to fight, racing*
their ponies between the
river and the column, ~~~~ but only a few long distance shots were exchanged.

Tuesday morning there was not an Indian anywhere.

The Gibbon-Terry force continued up the valley and presently
~~observed a number of curious~~ objects on the slope east of the river.
These objects appeared to be buffalo carcasses, ~~some~~ of which had
been skinned. Gibbon's chief of scouts, Lt. James Bradley, crossed
the river to find out what they were.

Soon afterward the column marched into an area that *obviously*
had ~~~~ been a huge Indian encampment.

3a.

3b.

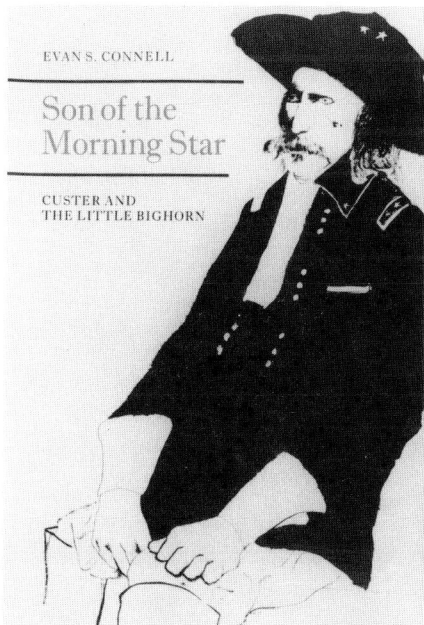

3. The typescript dated 4/27/81 is an early version of Son of the Morning Star. Its first page shows both the work's preliminary title, Broken Hoop, and a pair of epigraphs that Connell would eventually drop. The notations in the left-hand margins refer to the books from which Connell drew his information. Though designated "Third Draft," Connell explains, this "in fact might be the tenth or fifteenth time I wrote that page, and probably the previous drafts were cannibalized." The line cutting vertically down the page is Connell's indication that he has finished with this draft and begun work on a new one.

After several later versions of the manuscript, Connell arrived at the "Final Draft" that he submitted to his agent. But the process of revision was not yet complete, for Connell was still making minor stylistic adjustments on the galley proofs from North Point Press.

Harriet Doerr

Harriet Doerr was born in Pasadena in 1910 and grew up in Southern California. At seventeen she travelled to Massachusetts to attend Smith College, but transferred to Stanford in 1928. Here she studied European history, before leaving the university a year and a half later when she married Albert Doerr, an engineer who had also been a student at Stanford.

In 1960, with their two children grown, she and her husband moved to a Mexican village, where they lived for most of the next twelve years. A few years after her husband's death in 1972, Doerr took up her children's challenge to complete her university education and, forty-seven years after dropping out, returned to Stanford in 1977.

While completing her major in European history, Doerr also enrolled in an undergraduate creative writing class with John L'Heureux and began submitting impressions and memories of her years in Mexico. "As you grow old you accumulate ideas and eventually want to fish some of them out of the pool," she explains. "You want to pull things together—work the fragments into something." After receiving her bachelor's degree in 1977, Doerr continued to develop her fictional renderings of Mexico in postgraduate workshops. On the basis of several of these pieces, she was awarded a Stegner Fellowship in 1979. When a group of her Mexican stories won the *Transatlantic Review* - Henfield Foundation Award in 1982, Viking senior editor Corlies Smith became interested in publishing the larger manuscript from which they had been selected. The result was the novel *Stones for Ibarra*, which was released in 1984 when Doerr was seventy-three and honored the same year with the American Book Award for First Fiction.

Stones for Ibarra tells the story of a middle-aged couple who leave California to live in a small town on Mexico's central plateau. Sara and Richard Everton come to Ibarra to reopen the copper mine that Richard's family abandoned during the Mexican revolution of 1910. Ironically, as Richard brings new economic life to the town, he learns that he is fatally ill. Both Evertons respond to the news by throwing themselves fully into the activities of Ibarra. Richard devotes himself to the mine, while Sara studies the language, history, and traditions of the town. As Sara watches the townspeople, however, she senses that barriers of custom, idiom, and reserve will always lie between her and them. What she cannot know she must imagine, so that in the end her stories are "half heard and half invented." Sara's imagination renders Ibarra in vivid colors, which mask her feelings about her husband's illness. As his condition worsens, her stories show Ibarra growing more beautiful and the lives of its townpeople ever more passionate, until eventually her fictional world collapses under the emotional weight of her husband's imminent death:

> Until this moment she had refused to consider the sort of future that included hospital rooms and nurses, that threatened emergencies and an ambulance. She had denied a whole vocabulary of words: radiation, transfusion, hemorrhage. Until today she had convinced herself Richard might be spared them all.
>
> Standing here at noon on the long covered porch . . . she relinquished her right to have her way. None of it would happen as she had willed it. The magic pill would not be found. Richard would not recover.

Although many of the novel's details recall Doerr's own experiences in Mexico, she says *Stones for Ibarra* "is not an autobiographical novel and it is not about one place." In fact, Ibarra is an amalgamation of several mining towns Doerr saw while living in Mexico. "All you can write about is what you know," she explains, "but what you know is simply the foundation for all the rest, the important part, which is what you imagine." Indeed, *Stones for Ibarra* is a beautiful mix of precise description and poetic imagination. As Julie Salamon of the *Wall Street Journal* noted, Doerr "has created a world filled with extraordinary images and characters in language so fine you want to linger over each paragraph, each word."

Since the publication of *Stones for Ibarra*, Doerr continues to write fiction based in Mexico. One of the elements that still draws Doerr's imagination to Mexico is her respect for its people. "It's hard to say that you know another people well," Doerr says, but "I'm fascinated by Mexicans. They have a stoicism that isn't grim, a flair, an inner happiness that we have somehow lost." "They are wise," she adds. "They accept adversity as the common lot of mankind." While this theme is central to *Stones for Ibarra*, it is also present in her short story, "Picnic at Amapolas," which appeared in the *New Yorker* in 1986. Here an American man and woman meet in a La Luz real estate office. Both are running away from their pasts and have come to Mexico to buy land and start over. The two Americans with their psychology of escape and renewal contrast sharply with the Mexicans, who cling to their ancestral place. In the stark landscape and behind the scarred adobe walls of Amapolas, the Americans discern its history of poverty, drought, and violence, but they can also recognize the people's astonishing capacity for endurance, and their unassailable pride.

Doerr is now working on a new novel. "I have started another book about Mexico," she explains. "It's set in a different place, and the story and characters are different. I chose the setting after seeing it not far from a road I used to drive along. There's a pond or a small lake with some houses and a church reflected in it. I think I remember a circle of hills. In any case, I've seen all I need. I'll imagine the rest."

The lapse of fifty years between my entering and graduating from college wrongly suggests that I am of a leisurely nature. Nowhere else in my endeavors has this proved true, particularly in writing, which becomes increasingly less leisurely in the fierce glare of the actuarial tables.

When I came back to Stanford after forty-seven years, I applied for a class being taught by John L'Heureux, director of the writing program.

On a late spring morning I approached his office and knocked.

"Come in," said the director, and I pushed the door open a few timid inches and submitted at arm's length the three required stories. These he deposited without glance or comment on his desk.

"It's twelve o'clock," he said. "Shall we have lunch?"

We ate cottage cheese and peaches out of cartons under an oak tree at the student union and, while we ate, discussed go-go dancing and, in a separate context, sin. After mutual agreement on its definition, we turned to grace. But there is no easy way to say what grace is, even for a person who studied at a seminary. Eleven years later I still occasionally ask the director, "In a few simple words, what is grace?" And again he tries to explain.

This, however, is the only area in which John L'Heureux has failed to help. In graduate fiction classes, in conferences, in argumentative sessions concerned with the writing and rewriting of *Stones for Ibarra*, he has successfully explained everything, from the control of image and metaphor, to the perils of flashback, to the imperative of fearless cuts.

In thankful retrospect I see it was his lead my fellow students followed when they accepted my anachronistic presence in the class.

Harriet Doerr

Selected Works by Harriet Doerr

Fiction

Stones For Ibarra. New York: Viking, 1984.

Individual Interview

"A First Novelist at 73," with Herbert Mitgang. New York Times Book Review, 8 January 1984.

1. *In 1985* Ladies' Home Journal *asked Harriet Doerr to describe a special memory of summer for their July issue. The result was "Low Tide at Four," an account of a tranquil California summer day in 1939. Although only about six hundred words long, the piece is an excellent example of Doerr's elaborate processes of composition and revision.*

In the first draft, Doerr begins sketching the scene in longhand. As she describes her family's walk to the beach, the image of an approaching messenger intrudes upon her imagination. "Here is Mr. Bray," she writes in parentheses in the center of the sixth page, "the station agent, walking across the sand with a telegram." Using the verso of the previous page, Doerr then begins to flesh out this encounter, organizing the sequence of her thought with arrows. She also places question marks next to phrases and words that she will reconsider during later drafts. This pattern of narrative and fragments of dialogue, connected with arrows and scored with question marks, occurs throughout the seven pages of the first draft. By the time Doerr completes her fifth and final version, only a few elements of this first sketch remain.

1a.

1b.

2. The second, third, and fourth drafts of Doerr's memoir are all typescripts overlaid with intricate handwritten annotations. On the fourth page of the second draft, Doerr continues to develop the Mr. Bray passage, cutting lines from the typed version and introducing new elements by hand. Question marks occur in both type and longhand, again highlighting problematic words, while asterisks mark places where Doerr will add the new phrases sketched in the margins. In the center of the page, she breaks the prose with dashes, indicating her intention to introduce a transitional paragraph that provisionally begins, "I read, and." At this point in the next draft, Doerr inserts a list of the books that she read on the beach during the summer of 1939; she also introduces a wholly new section on Mrs. Winfield's arrival.

In the final two drafts of "Low Tide at Four," Doerr introduces an element of menace into the tranquil day. The fourth draft includes the image of a Marine fighter plane flying dangerously low over the beach. This is the first intimation of the era's political turbulence. Then, while editing her final draft by typewriter, Doerr expands a stranger's comment on the times to include the question, "How about that paperhanger, Adolf?," alluding directly to Hitler and the imminent war in Europe. By indicating the historical setting of this summer day, Doerr gives the reader insight into why the memory persists so strongly for her. It was a peaceful interlude that would soon be shattered by World War II.

4

and our hearts sink at the prospect of their arrival, particularly
in the afternoon, particularly at the time of low tide.

"Stay on the beach for a while," we tell Mr. Bray. But
he has to get back to his station, which is just across the
tracks from Mrs. Tustin's pergola, and see to his trains. A
streamliner has lately been added to the run. (line?)
When it passes, everyone, regardless of age, turns to look.
The afternoon passes. The children, with splashes of wet
sand in their hair, dig trenches at the tide's slow edge. Their
father walks out to the end of the pier, to catch a wave, rides it
in, and walks out again to catch another. I swim, then come
back to the umbrella shade to read, then swim and read again.
The salt water drying, the air on my skin, the blue afternoon
on my knee.
the book

—————— I read, and ——————

At four o'clock, we are standing all together in shallow
water at low tide. The childred stand in one place and sink
deeper with every wave. The water is thick with grains of
gold sand. The children's skins have turned every shade of
honey, orange blossom, clover, desert. Now they
are buckwheat. Everything stops for a moment. long enough for
the sun to hang where it is for a second, for the furthest foam
of the lowest wave to hesitate. For me to look at my husband
over the children's heads. Time to think, yes, magic.

2

pergola. Instead, we carry them, along with towels, buckets,
shovels, books, and an umbrella, down the perilous, tilting
wooden stairs to the beach. Later, we go back to the pergola
for chocolate and vanilla cones.

"Ice cream special, cherry mint ripple," says Mrs. Tustin
on this particular day, and we watch a fat man lick a scoop
of it from his cone. We wait for him to say, "Not bad," or
"I'll try anything once," but he has no comment. A long freight
train rattles by on the tracks behind the pergola.

As we turn away, Mrs. Tustin says, "The world's in big
that paperhanger, Adolf?"
trouble," and the fat man says, "You can say that again. How about/
But it is hard to hear because of the train.

Back on the beach, our heads under the umbrella, we
The sun hangs hot and high.
lie at compass points like a four-pointed star. / Small gusts
of wind lift the children's corn-straw hair. We taste salt.
Face down, arms wide, we cling to the revolving earth.

Now Mr. Bray, the station agent, a middle-aged Mercury
in a shiny suit, crosses the dry sand in his leather shoes.
He is delivering a telegram. Everyone listens while I read
them the message from our best and oldest friends. Sorry,
they can't come next weekend, after all. Good, we say to
ourselves, without shame.

I invite Mr. Bray to join us under the umbrella. "Can't
you stay on the beach for a while?" He pauses with sand
sifting into his shoes. Oh, no, he has to get back to his
his trains. He left his wife on charge and the new Diesel
streamliner will be coming through.

2a.

2b.

Ernest J. Gaines

Ernest J. Gaines was born in 1933 on a sugar cane plantation near Baton Rouge, Louisiana, where his family had lived and worked for five generations. When he was fifteen he moved with his mother and stepfather to San Francisco and out of loneliness began reading fiction in the local library. "But the books I read," says Gaines, "did not have my people in them, no Southern blacks, Louisiana blacks." And the more he read, the greater his desire to see the Louisiana world of his childhood represented in fiction. "I wanted to see on paper those black parents going to work before the sun came up and coming back home to look after their children after the sun went down...I wanted to see on paper the small country churches... and I wanted to hear those simple religious songs, those simple prayers—that true devotion." At sixteen, Gaines dedicated himself to becoming a writer of the Louisiana landscape.

Gaines completed high school in California and after two years of military service attended San Francisco State College. While there, he worked on a novel, but when it was turned down for publication, he burned it. In 1958 he was awarded a Stegner Fellowship in fiction. At Stanford, Gaines concentrated on short stories, but a New York editor who visited the writing seminar warned him that there was no money in shorter forms. "I thought I'd never have a penny when I left Stanford," Gaines remembers, so he returned to the subject matter of the novel he had earlier destroyed. He gave himself ten years to succeed in his craft, while earning his living through odd jobs at the post office and a printing shop. In 1964, after just five years, his resurrected book, now titled *Catherine Carmier,* was accepted for publication, and Gaines has devoted himself to writing ever since.

In the two novels and the collection of stories that Gaines published in the 1960s, he introduces the fictional town of Bayonne, Louisiana, which remains the geographic center of his work. These early books explore the strained and passionate lives of his bayou country people. *Catharine Carmier* tells the story of a woman whose life is dominated by her relationship with her father, while Gaines's second novel, *Of Love and Dust* (1967), recounts a doomed love affair between a rebellious black man and a white woman. Both books examine the intricate interplay of commitment, desire, and violence in contemporary Louisiana, but they left Gaines dissatisfied. When "*Of Love and Dust* was finished," he says, "I realized that I had done only a small part of what I had intended to write." In his close focus on the contemporary he had neglected the historical background that conditions his characters. To evoke these other layers of motivation Gaines found himself "going farther and farther back into the past. I was trying to go back, back, back into our experiences in this country to find some kind of meaning to our present lives."

This deeper search into the Louisiana past produced in 1971 the work that won Gaines wide critical acclaim. In *The Autobiography of Miss Jane Pittman* he invents a world spanning nearly a century. The book chronicles the social and political transitions in Louisiana from the Civil War to the days of Martin Luther King, as they affect the life of Gaines's fictional heroine. Through Miss Pittman's memories, the novel dramatically reenacts the South's troubled past and projects the promise of racial reconciliation. Through her eyes the reader gains insight into the trials and faiths of an entire people. It is a testament to the power of Gaines's imagination that *Newsweek* wrote to him and asked for a photograph of Miss Pittman to accompany its review.

In 1978 Gaines published his fourth novel, *In My Father's House.* Though set in the present, its major concern is a problem in black American culture that originates in the slave trade. The book relates the story of Phillip Martin, a respected minister and civil rights leader. At the height of Martin's influence, his son from younger, wanton days arrives in town, reminding the minister of old commitments and betrayals. For Gaines, the tensions that arise between the father and his abandoned son typify the breakdown of parentage rooted in the black American past. "Blacks were taken out of Africa," says Gaines, "and separated traditionally and then physically here in this country...mothers were separated from their children, husbands from their wives, fathers from their sons, mothers from their daughters. And I feel that because of that separation they still have not, philosophically speaking, reached each other again."

Gaines's greatest stylistic achievement is his most recent novel, *A Gathering of Old Men* (1983). It opens with the shooting death of a young Cajun man known for strong-arming the black community. By the time the local sheriff arrives, however, nearly twenty old black men have gathered around the body with shotguns, each claiming that he pulled the trigger. For the old men, a hundred years of degradation condense into a single moment of defiance. But what is most compelling about Gaines's rendition of the story is that it is told by fifteen separate narrators, both black and white, who participate in the events of the day. Their multiple perspectives allow us to draw distinctions and comparisons among the pride, anger, and courage of the individual blacks and whites involved. Through these highly personal accounts Gaines gives voice to the history of antagonism and the promise of equality in Bayonne. But even with the completion of *A Gathering of Old Men,* Gaines remains dissatisfied. "Because you always feel that you've failed," he says, "and that you did not say in this book all that you wanted to say.... So you never really finish. Not if you are a writer. All you do is go to the next book."

I think each book is a part of the big book. It's like a chapter. As you write, you discover new things, and each book that you go through only adds more questions. So you try to answer those questions in the next book. But by the time you get to that book and go through it, you reach the same thing again. You answer some questions, but other questions arise.

I think that the entire thing about writing is that you're constantly searching but never finding the answer. Because you discover two questions for every answer that you find. It's a continual process, and probably you never will get the answers together. And some one else will just pick up the baton after you and continue the relay race. At least you hope that's what happens.

In *A Gathering of Old Men* I was trying to bring out the heroic character of men who have suffered all kind of iniquities most of their lives, and one day they just want to stand in the sun-- which is the story of all men, of all races, of all times. What I was dealing with in *A Gathering of Old Men* was a race of men, a race who have suffered these iniquities and found a way to stand one day. They found a reason to stand one day around their friend Mathu. But they were men standing for individual reasons as well, for their own reasons. They all had a reason, not a reason to shoot a Fix or shoot Beau, but they'd all suffered, they'd all had injustice done to them, and so whoever did pull the trigger, every other man there could have done that one time in his life, or probably wished he had, or wished if not with a gun, but stood up some kind of way.

Although I'd say ninety percent of everything in *A Gathering of Old Men* is fictional, I started with factual things. For example, one day I was visiting this old man, whom I called Mathu in the book. I used to visit him whenever I'd go to Louisiana. And he'd be the first person I'd go out to the country to see, at the old place where I'd grown up as a child until I was fifteen years old, and came to California. I remember, this man was in his nineties, he had I don't know how many children and probably a hundred grandchildren, and he is known to be a good fisherman and hunter and all kinds of things, and I remember, he and I were talking on his porch one day when a white guy started arguing with an older black man a little bit further down the road, just across the road from where we were. And I could see by the way this man was looking at this, I could see how much he didn't like it; but he never did say anything to me about it. I could see by his face that he didn't like what was going on.

I also know someone somewhat like the character Candy, and as a matter of fact she's still there on that plantation, she's part owner of it. Mathu in my book really is a combination of two or three actual people and I remember when one of these men died how much she cried. Because this man had sort of looked after her, and she was very close to him. He had been born there and he was in his middle or late eighties when he died. And she had known him from a child, had grown up knowing about this man, seeing this man just about every day of her life. I remember when she heard of his death she called my telephone in Lafeyette, but I was in Baton Rouge. So she left a message on my answering machine, she was crying about this man's death. So I knew her feelings about this particular man, and others around her.

I start with these factual things, then after a while I begin to fictionalize them, but I'm still talking about the old places, the old place, the old people and their attitudes. Because you deal with attitudes. Everybody in *A Gathering of Old Men* is living in the past. Candy lives in the past, the old men and the Fixes live in the past, and Mapes, of course, lives in the past. He thinks if he just comes in and slaps people around they're going to confess, they're going to put one person up to be slaughtered, as sheriffs have done in the past. So it takes Gil, and others, younger men, working together in sports or whatever to try to make a little change, and they're the only ones we can look forward to making changes because the old ones I feel will not make the changes, the old ones are so ingrained into those attitudes about race and whatever else.

Ernest J. Gaines

Excerpts from a conversation, July 1988

Selected Works by Ernest J. Gaines

Fiction

Catherine Carmier. New York: Atheneum, 1964.
Of Love and Dust. New York: Dial Press, 1967.
Bloodline. New York: Dial Press, 1968.
The Autobiography of Miss Jane Pittman. New York: Dial Press, 1971.
In My Father's House. New York: Knopf, 1978.
A Gathering of Old Men. New York: Knopf, 1983.

Individual Interviews

"Ernest Gaines: A Conversation," with Paul Desruisseaux. *New York Times Book Review*, 11 June 1978.
"Ernest J. Gaines—'Other Things to Write About,'" with Mary Ellen Doyle. *Melus*, Summer 1984.
Fiction!: Interviews with Northern California Novelists, with Dan Tooker and Roger Hofheins. New York: Harcourt Brace Jovanovich, 1976.
"This Louisiana Thing that Drives Me: An Interview with Ernest J. Gaines," with Charles H. Rowell. *Callaloo*, 1.3 (1978).

Ernest J. Gaines began *A Gathering of Old Men* as a story told entirely from the perspective of Lou Dimes, a liberal white reporter. But after a year of writing, he says, "I realized that Dimes could not get all the information needed and especially not the language I wanted: the child's or the old women's. . .or the men fishing." At that point, Gaines radically reorganized the novel, retelling the story from fifteen different points of view and enriching the tale by affording a variety of narrative voices.

1. Gaines writes his novels in three separate stages. He first works in longhand, often moving through several drafts as he defines the structure of the story. For this initial stage, Gaines always uses cheap yellow paper, a habit that goes back to his days as a mail clerk in 1957. It was the only office paper available to him, and he has relied on it ever since.

After the story line coheres, Gaines then switches to typescript and revises again, concentrating on the rhythms of the language and the dialogue. This second stage may also undergo several drafts. In the third stage, which Gaines calls his first draft, he types a manuscript for his agent. For many years this was Dorothea Oppenheimer, whom Gaines acknowledges as his most helpful editor and critic. Displayed here are examples of the first two stages, the longhand and the typescript with revisions.

1a.

"I think I do," Mapes said. "I'm sure I do."

"Then wh don't you arrest him?"

"They all kk say the same thing. They all claim they did it."

"But you know who did it?"

"Yes," Mapes said. "I know who did it. But the others threatened to come to town if I take him. She says the same thing. I don't want this crowd in Bayonne. Not with people getting ready for that game tomorrow."

"So what do lyou plan to do, Mapes?"

"I'll handle it."

"You haven't done it yet. My brothr been dead, how long, four hours?"

"Three or four," Mapes said.

Gil looked at him. Mapes looked away. Gil continued to look at him a while longer be ore he turned to look at the old men wit the guns. His eyes finally settled on the one nearest the steps. He was tall, skinny, and very black, as black as you can get. His reddish, brown eyes looked the same color old water looks in rivers. He was the only one there with a doublebarrell shotgun. The gun was clasped under his right arm, with the barrell pointed toward the ground. He looked straight back at Gil. He didn't lower his eyes the way they were supposed to do when a white man stared at them. None of the other old gentlemen lowered their eyes either. You could see how much a strain it was on them to hold themselves erect like that, but they were sure trying to do a good job of it.

"You, Mathu?" Gil said.

"Yes."

Gil had said it as if he had known without a doubt that it would be this one and no one else. And the old man answered him simple and direct. He did not answer with bitterness. He dad answered the same way he probably would have answerd you if you

JANICE ROBINSON

a k a

Janey

Lord have mercy, Jesus, what now? Where do I turn? Go where first? The Major? For what? He's already drunk out there on that front garry, and it's just twelve o'clock. Miss Bea? That's like talking to the wall. Where? Mr. Lou? Yes. She said call Mr. Lou. Mr. Lou and Miss Merle. I better make it Mr. Lou first. Lord, have mercy, keep me on my feet if it is thy holy will.

I went in and dialed the paper in Baton Rouge—my finger trembling, just a-trembling. When the operator answered, I told her I wanted to speak to Mr. Lou Dimes. She told me that was "City," and told me to hold on. Then somebody else answered and said, "City"; then he said, "Toby Wright." I told him I wanted to speak to Mr. Lou Dimes. "Lou at dinner right now," he said. "Oh, Lord," I said. "Where? Find him. Hurry. Candy want him here right away. Please, sir. Please." "Just hold on," he said. "Calm down. He'll be back in a little while. Who am I speaking to? That's you, Janey?" "Yes, sir, it's me," I said. "Find him fast as you can, and tell him get here fast as he can. He don't have to call. Just get here. And please hurry. Hurry."

2. The heart of Gaines's fiction is its dialogue and the musical qualities of its narrative. "In dialogue and narrative there must be a rhythmic flow at all times," Gaines says. "When a story is told from the first-person point of view, the narrator does not only give facts, but he or she must give that information in his or her own peculiar way—depending on education, social background, age, sex, race, Christian or non-Christian, whatever. Much more than by action or description, my characters are defined by the way they speak, by their choice of words and how those words are strung together. This is the music I speak of."

Referring to the narrator of the second chapter, Gaines comments, "Janey's style of speaking in refrains, saying something and then answering herself, is typical of gospel music in black churches." The modulations that distinguish her voice typify the role of music throughout Gaines's writing. As he explains, "I have learned as much about writing about my people by listening to blues and jazz and spirituals as I have learned by reading."

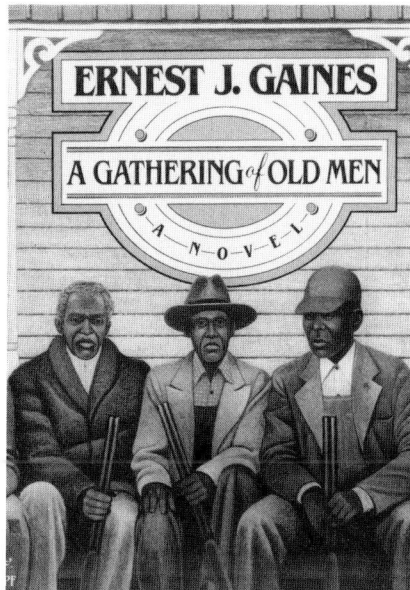

ERNEST J. GAINES

A GATHERING of OLD MEN

A NOVEL

Thom Gunn

Thom Gunn inhabits the present with a restless intensity that makes his poetry one of our most authentic records of the changing moods and shifting values of postwar urban society. "It is a strange fact," he explains, "that almost everything that figures importantly in my life, an event, an idea, even a series of dreams, finds its way sooner or later into poetry." But though autobiography provides the sources of his art, Gunn scrupulously avoids exploiting his personality. For him, poetry is not a forum for feverish confession or moral posturing, but an instrument to advance his own and his readers' understanding of the contemporary human moment.

Born in Gravesend, Kent, in 1929, Gunn grew up predominantly in the London suburb of Hampstead. The family, though largely exempt from the economic hardships of Depression England, suffered its own private tragedies: the divorce of Gunn's parents before he was ten and the death of his mother five years later. She was an avid reader who taught him that books are "not just a commentary on life but a part of its continuing activity." It was for his mother's birthday that Gunn wrote his first long work, "a curiously sophisticated" comic novel called *The Flirt*. At the time he was only twelve and staying in Hampshire, away from London and the ravages of the Blitz. When Gunn returned to London, he lived with aunts and family friends while completing school. Two years' National Service in the British army preceded his going up to read English at Trinity College, Cambridge in 1950.

Gunn knew by age sixteen that he wanted to be a writer. He had, in fact, been working seriously but sporadically at novels and poems since 1945, though he invariably found the results "imitative and dispiriting." The problem, he explains, was that "my imagination retreated too easily into the world before my mother's death, a world that in practice excluded most of the twentieth century." Cambridge quickly changed him. There he became part of the ambitious, aggressively talented circle of undergraduates who edited the university's literary magazine. He also attended F. R. Leavis's legendary lectures and learned to appreciate Elizabethan and seventeenth-century poetry, particularly John Donne, whose passionate involvement in his own times opened Gunn's imagination fully to the present. What emerged from these Cambridge years were the poems gathered in his first major book, *Fighting Terms*, published in July of 1954, just after his graduation. Adapting Donne's metaphysical style to contemporary subject matter, Gunn produced irreverently realistic, tightly controlled verse that caught the new temper of toughness in postwar Britain. This anti-romantic stance immediately led critics to associate Gunn with the Movement, a group of conservative, slightly older British writers, including Philip Larkin, Kingsley Amis, and Donald Davie, all of whom shared Gunn's distaste for sentimentality and his attraction to traditional poetic forms.

But Gunn's alliance with the Movement was more critical fabrication than fact, a point underscored two months after the appearance of *Fighting Terms*, when he left England to study in the Stanford Creative Writing Program under Yvor Winters. Though Gunn soon decided that Winters's conception of a poem was "too rigid, excluding in practice much of what I could not but consider good poetry," his year in Palo Alto was nonetheless very productive. He wrote steadily, including "To Yvor Winters, 1955," an eloquent tribute to his teacher's personal warmth, moral seriousness, and love of poetry. He also began to study the American modernist poets, particularly Wallace Stevens and William Carlos Williams, who would play an increasingly vital role in his development.

Many of the poems Gunn wrote during the 1954-55 academic year at Stanford were included in his second collection, *The Sense of Movement* (1957), a book characterized by a tense mixture of Sartrean philosophy, popular culture, and conservative poetic forms. In the language of existentialism, Gunn exalts wild, often intimidating characters whose anarchic energy pushes them to the margins of society. Masculine will, bravado, self-regarding power—these qualities dominate.

By the time *The Sense of Movement* appeared, Gunn was again at Stanford, no longer attending Winters's workshops but enrolled instead in the English Department's doctoral program. The next year, before taking a graduate degree, he left to accept a post at the University of California at Berkeley, where he still teaches part-time. Gunn's fondness for northern California and his special love for San Francisco, born of his first visit to the city in 1954, had now evolved into a permanent attachment, and he made the city his home. But in the late 1950s, Gunn became less certain about his poetry. The first two books, he came to realize, had depended too heavily on "blustering heroism...as if there were no other way of getting outside oneself." A less aggressive, more generous stance was necessary, if his work was to break out of its narrow circle of formal artifice and conscious control into different areas of experience.

What followed in *My Sad Captains* (1961) were the first signs of Gunn's more "humane impulse," as he characterized his new direction. The volume's title poem beautifully captures this tone. Thematically, it bids farewell to those remote, "hard energy" heroes that dominated Gunn's earlier books, while stylistically, it moves with an improvisational freedom impossible within traditional forms. *My Sad Captains* also records Gunn's deepening feelings for the physical world—no longer does the California landscape threaten human efforts to achieve personal meaning. As the liberating idealism and infectious optimism of San Francisco in the 1960s penetrated Gunn's sensibility, his openness to people and nature became an ecstatic embrace. The title poem of his next major book, *Touch* (1967), celebrates an erotic communion that releases lovers into the "dark/wide realm where we/walk with everyone," while the poems in *Moly* (1971) testify to the spiritual power of human love and natural beauty.

As the euphoria of the early 1960s gave way to the politics of Vietnam and the anxieties of the 1970s, elements of melancholy and reserve reasserted themselves in Gunn's writing. The title sequence of *Jack Straw's Castle* (1976) originated in a nightmare that haunted Gunn for months. Recalling the claustrophobic solipsism of the early work, the poem deals, Gunn explains, "with the terrors of self-destructiveness you may face when you are aware of being trapped in your own skull." But Gunn refuses to allow this somber mood to erase the beatific dreams of the 1960s. "Everything that we glimpsed," he argues, "the trust, the brotherhood, the repossession of innocence, the nakedness of spirit—is still a possibility and will continue to be so."

Gunn's most recent large-scale collection, *Passages of Joy* (1982), sustains this tension between the positive and negative poles of human possibility. In fact, the volume's title inscribes Gunn's ambivalent vision. In the context of the Samuel Johnson poem from which he draws it, the phrase resonates with the decay of the flesh and the inevitability of death; but Gunn also uses Johnson's words literally to refer to sexual pleasures. Since his Cambridge days, these have centered for Gunn in homosexual companionship, and both *Passages of Joy* and the new booklet, *The Hurtless Trees* (1986), address this aspect of his life more candidly than ever before. The latest verse, at once accessible, energetic, and engagingly honest, again extends Gunn's poetic reach. The daring of its tone and form recalls his abiding wish "not [to] have the risk diminished." It is precisely this encompassing of both the dangers and the promises of our contemporary world that renders Gunn's poetry so valuable.

Certainly my year as a writing fellow at Stanford was one of the most important in my life. Now, in 1988, I call myself an Anglo-American poet: I was raised largely in London, and 1954-5 was my first year in America, and so it was the hinge on which my life was to open.

I landed in New York, and from there came across the country by train, to enter San Francisco on the ferry from Oakland, a prepossessing approach. San Francisco was still a low-built city, less grandiose and more comfortable-looking than it is today: its first high-rise was not to be put up until the end of that decade. It was not like anywhere I had ever seen before; and now that I live here, I find it small enough to manage but large enough to offer all the variety a fast walker could want.

Stanford, too, was different from what it is today. A lot of the campus that is now built up was still dusty bush and eucalyptus. Now there are so many new buildings that I tend to become lost on it. I used to sit in the sun by the steps of the old library reading William Carlos Williams and Wallace Stevens and the other poets that Yvor Winters said I ought to read to further my education.

It was all I knew of the United States then, anyway, what I saw around me at Stanford or on my trips to San Francisco, Yvor Winters and Janet Lewis, blue jays on the campus and motorcyclists on El Camino, kids playing up and down the steps of the Frost Amphitheater in their Davey Crockett caps, and in back of the Peninsula towns many orchards crowded beneath the blond bare hills. It all seemed to promise great richness of experience, and I must say I have not been disappointed, though I could never have foreseen quite how rich and varied the experience of the next thirty-four years was to be.

I lived in a top room at 334 Lincoln Avenue, for which the rent was only $15 a month (the good Mrs. Hyde had never asked more in the previous decades, and she didn't see why she should now); it was a shingled house with squirrels jumping on the roof from nearby trees—I could see them only a few feet away, through the window, from the table where I wrote. There I wrote the bulk of my second book of poetry, *The Sense of Movement*, and my life started to swing open upon a new country.

I wrote "On the Move" in the spring of 1955. Much of it derives, quite self-consciously, from Sartre's lecture "L'Existentialisme est un Humanisme," which I had been reading. I was excited while writing it, because I could see it as my biggest poem to date, i.e. including more of the world, of my experience, than I had managed to get into any other poem. New connections kept making themselves, new ambitions kept declaring themselves.

Thom Gunn

Selected Works by Thom Gunn

Poetry

Fighting Terms. Oxford: Fantasy Press, 1954; revised edition, New York: Hawk's Well Press, 1958.
The Sense of Movement. London: Faber and Faber, 1957; Chicago: University of Chicago Press, 1959.
My Sad Captains and Other Poems. London: Faber and Faber, 1961; Chicago: University of Chicago Press, 1961.
Selected Poems, with Ted Hughes. London: Faber and Faber, 1962.
Positives, photographs by Ander Gunn. London: Faber, 1966; Chicago: University of Chicago Press, 1967.
Touch. London: Faber, 1967; Chicago: University of Chicago Press, 1968.
Poems 1950-1966: A Selection. London: Faber, 1969.
Moly. London: Faber, 1971.
Jack Straw's Castle. London: Faber, 1976; New York: Farrar Straus Giroux, 1976.
Selected Poems 1950-1975. London: Faber, 1979; New York: Farrar Straus Giroux, 1979.
The Passages of Joy. London: Faber, 1982; New York: Farrar Straus Giroux, 1982.
The Hurtless Trees. New York: Jordan Davies, 1986.

Other

The Occasions of Poetry: Essays in Criticism and Autobiography. London: Faber, 1982; New York: Farrar Straus Giroux, 1982.

Editor, *Selected Poems of Fulke Greville.* London: Faber, 1968; Chicago: University of Chicago Press, 1968.
Editor, *Ben Jonson.* London: Penguin, 1974.

Individual Interviews

"Gunn in America," with W.I. Scobie. *London Magazine,* December 1977.
Talking Poetry: Conversations in the Workshop with Contemporary Poets, with Lee Bartlett. Albuquerque: University of New Mexico Press, 1987.
Viewpoints: Poets in Conversation, with John Haffenden. London: Faber, 1981.

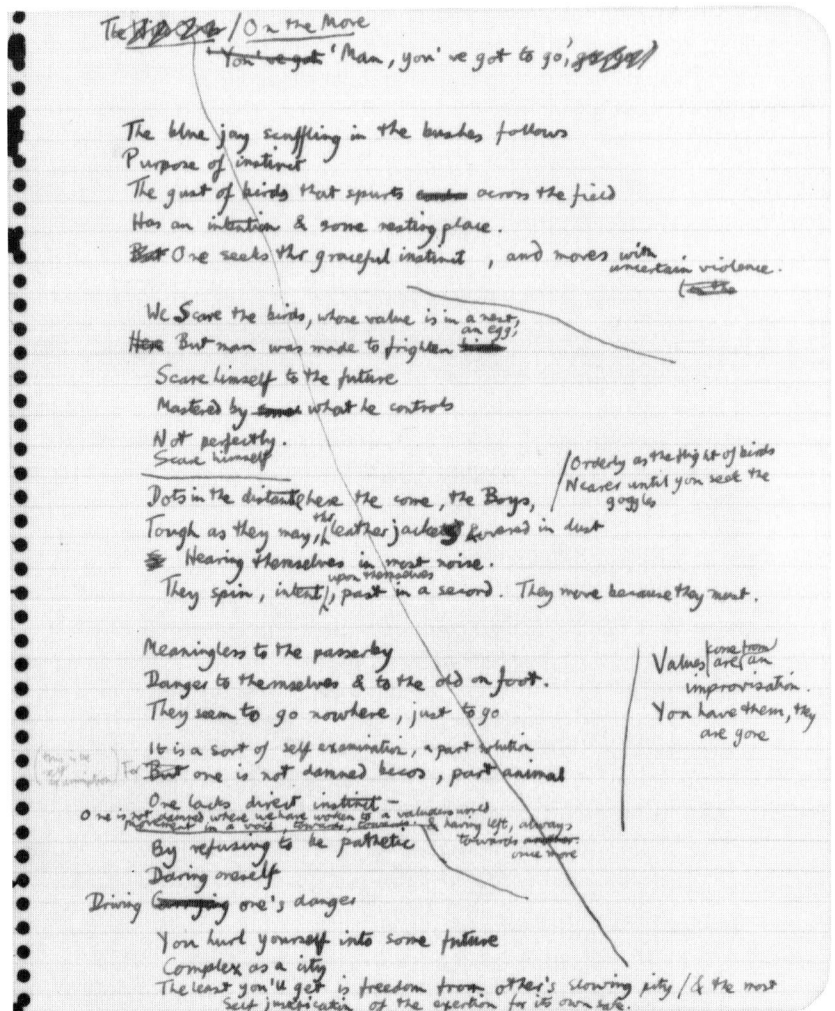

1.

"The thing you want to write about," Gunn explains in a recent interview, "gestates, and the process of writing becomes an exploration. You discover things about yourself and about your insight into your subject matter that you didn't even guess at. The surprises that occur on the way are often the most exciting things about writing." Twenty-five densely revised drafts in both manuscript and typescript testify to Gunn's complex process of discovery as it evolved for the poem, "On the Move," which was written from March to May of 1955 when he lived in Palo Alto and participated in Yvor Winters's poetry workshops. First published in the December 1955 issue of Encounter and then featured as the opening piece in his second book, The Sense of Movement (1957), the poem reflects Gunn's fascination with "the American myth of the motorcyclist." In the tough, solitary and often violent life of this "wild man part free spirit and part hoodlum," Gunn saw a paradigm of modern existentialist fate.

1. In this earliest extant version of "On the Move," few of the poem's formal features are evident. Though the draft is divided into stanzas, these divisions remain quite rough, and there are only fitful hints of rhyme and metrical schemes. Gunn's efforts are concentrated on delineating basic images and aligning them along the poem's thematic axis. He carefully connects the blue jay with the instinctual order of nature, against which the motocyclists must rebel in their quest for a uniquely human universe. The annotations suggest that Gunn did not question the necessity of the individual's violent separation from nature but instead focused on the rebellion's dangers. One of the greatest of these risks is caught by a marginal note that reads, "Values are an improvisation," a statement that reinforces Gunn's other references here to a "meaningless," "valueless world."

On loan from the State University of New York at Buffalo

On the Move

'Man, you gotta Go.'

1. The blue jay scuffling in the bushes follows
Some hidden purpose, and the gust of birds
That spurts across the field, the wheeling swallows
Find a direction in the undergrowth.
Seeking their instinct, or their poise, or both
One moves with an uncertain violence
Under the dust thrown by a baffled sense
Thro dust thrown up(ward) by a baffled sense
& the dull thunder of approximate words.

['hidden' i.e. ordained]

/ Have found direction in the undergrowth
/ Have rested in the trees & undergrowth

2. Hovering in the heat, (mere) dots, at first,
They come, nearer and nearer, — the Boys
throws them forth, the burst
Until the distance yields them, (with) a burst
Of sound that thunder localised : (They agree)
That is that thunder localised. (They agree)
That thunder localised. — they agree
They localise that thunder. They agree

In goggles, donned impersonality,
In [leather] jackets [gleaming thro] [caked] dust
gleaming trophies with the

They / To strap in doubt; they move because they must,
hold

& almost hear a meaning in their noise.

in
a cry
defy
high
lie
the
thigh
dry
try
fly
shy
sky

2.

2. After several more manuscript versions, "On the Move" assumed many of its final features. In this intermediate draft, the familiar five-stanza structure is now securely in place, while both the abaccd-db rhyme scheme and the iambic metrical norm, lacking in the first draft, are set. Themes have also achieved sharper, more forceful articulation. In fact, two of this version's central statements—the third stanza's "Men manufacture both machine and soul," and the concluding line, "One is always nearer by not keeping still"—will continue unchanged into the published text.

Building on these advances, Gunn revises on several different levels. Especially conspicuous is his habit of listing in multiple-choice format alternative words, and even entire lines. In the second stanza, Gunn uses this method to identify the best rhyme word. Gunn also deals directly with the ideas governing "On the Move."

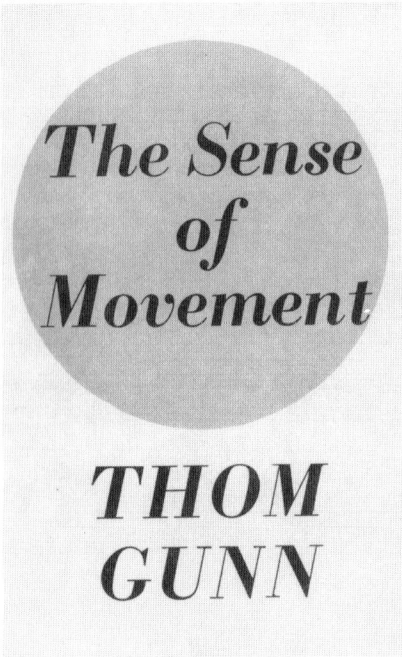

The Sense of Movement

THOM GUNN

3. After several more handwritten drafts, Gunn produced the first typescript of "On the Move." Though the poem's final state is easily perceptible here, Gunn remains dissatisfied with various local phrasings. Most are matters of rhythm and sound, but each affects the sense as well. Typical of Gunn's practice is the choice he entertains in the final stanza among four adjectives, "bursting," "troubled," "crowded," and "muddled." The four carry meanings sufficiently different both to change the significance of Gunn's city metaphor and to alter the texture of the poem as a whole.

Another kind of revision, occurring in the fifth stanza, is signalled by Gunn's marginal notes at the bottom right-hand side of the page. Here he proposes to extend the third stanza's reference to medieval knights into the poem's conclusion, by equating the Holy Grail's legendary elusiveness with the modern world's loss of absolutes.

On loan from the State University of New York at Buffalo

4. After the first typescript, Gunn rewrote "On the Move" six more times by hand before returning to a typed format--and then three further typescripts preceded this penultimate drafting. Except for a single line, the poem is now in its published state. The universalizing references to medieval knights, present since the earliest stages of composition, have been eliminated, thereby narrowing the poem's focus to contemporary culture. Most of the minor stylistic cruxes are also resolved.

But the rigor of Gunn's attention to formal matters remains very much in evidence. As his extensive annotations indicate, the rhythm of the final stanza's fourth line still bothered Gunn. Its awkwardness in the context of the poem's iambic norm provoked him to numerous renderings, in search of a combination of words to satisfy both sense and meter. In the end, Gunn chose neither of the alternatives he here designates "best yet" and "2nd best." Rather, he adopted the version that appears as the first note in the right-hand margin. With its classic iambic flow, the line, "Are home for neither bird nor holiness," not only sustains the stanza's rhythm but also adds another layer of connotation by introducing the highly resonant word "home."

On loan from the State University of New York at Buffalo

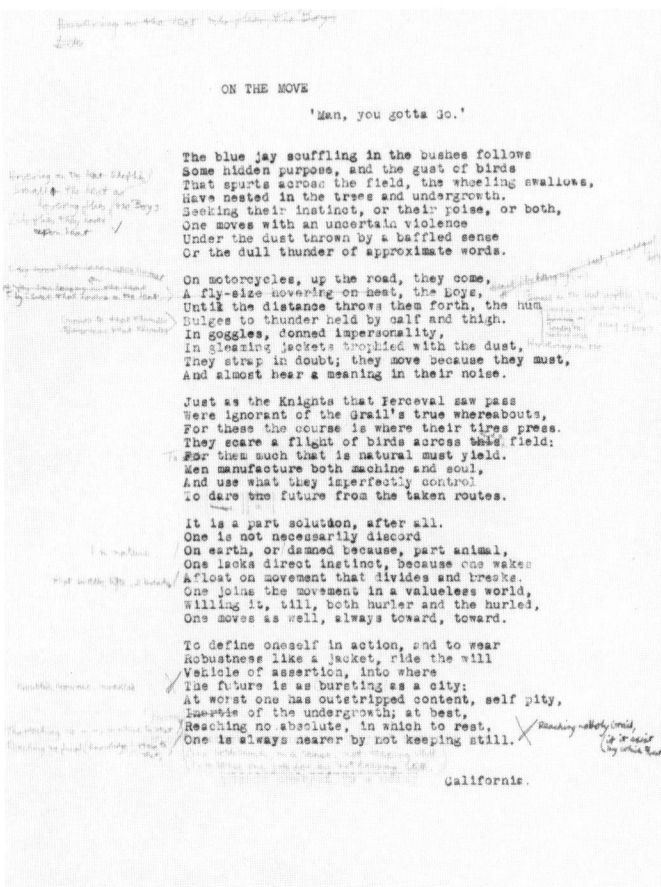

3.

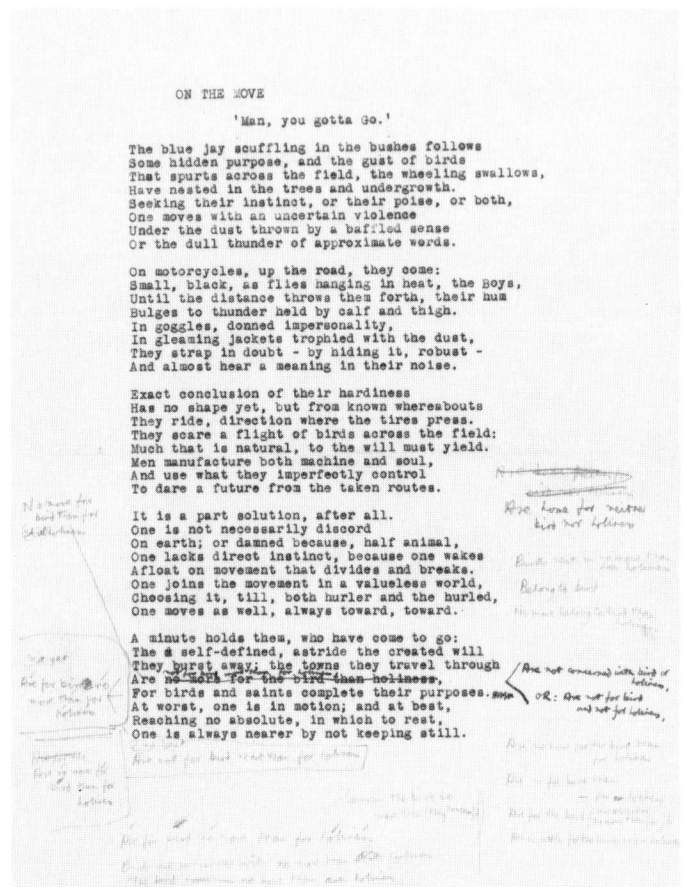

4.

Donald Hall

Born in 1928, Donald Hall grew up in the suburbs of New Haven, Connecticut, but spent Christmas holidays and summers at Eagle Pond in New Hampshire, where his mother's parents were old-fashioned one-horse farmers. The love and solitude Hall enjoyed on the family homestead made it the emotional and imaginative center of his life, "my own secret place," he calls it, "where I kept to myself and daydreamed." Hall wrote his first poems at twelve. By fourteen he was completely enthralled with poetry, and at sixteen he attended the Bread Loaf Writers' Conference, where he first met Robert Frost. While taking his undergraduate degree, he edited the *Harvard Advocate* and made personal contacts with other important writers, including Dylan Thomas and T. S. Eliot. These acquaintances Hall later recounted in *Remembering Poets* (1978), a tribute to the forebears of his own literary generation that Donald Davie declared "a modern classic." After studying for an advanced degree at Oxford, Hall returned to America in 1953 to spend a year with Yvor Winters in Stanford's Creative Writing Program. At this time he wrote much of *Exiles and Marriages* (1955), his first book of poems. Three years at Harvard as a junior fellow then preceded nineteen years as a professor of English at the University of Michigan. When Hall retired from that post in 1975, it was to move permanently to Eagle Pond, where he now lives with his wife, the poet Jane Kenyon.

In the three decades since he studied at Stanford, Hall has become an accomplished and versatile man of letters. His wide-ranging publications include a study of British sculptor Henry Moore, a biography of Major League baseball pitcher Dock Ellis, and a respected writing textbook now in its sixth edition. Among his children's stories, *The Ox-Cart Man* (1979) won the Caldecott Medal. But "poetry has remained," Hall says, "the center of my life." In addition to producing eight collections of his own poems, Hall is a prominent critic of contemporary poetry. This role began in 1953, when he became poetry editor for the *Paris Review,* and has continued through numerous anthologies, the influential *Poets on Poetry* series he initiated for the University of Michigan Press in 1978, and his frequent reviews and notes about fellow poets, now gathered into four volumes, *Goatfoot Milktongue Twinbird* (1978), *To Keep Moving* (1980), *The Weather for Poetry* (1982), and *Poetry and Ambition* (1988).

Lending coherence to this remarkable body of literary achievement is Donald Hall's distinctive sensibility. Rooted in childhood memories of his grandparents' New England farm, his temperament extends back into family history and down into the remoter recesses of the self, seeking an identity that is at once individual to him and common to his readers. Elegiac about the past but alert to the present, Hall combines conservative respect for tradition with radical openness to experience. The result is a generosity of spirit that is, perhaps, the defining quality of both his creative and his critical work.

A new contentment entered Hall's work after his return to Eagle Pond. In an interview he explains, "Now I feel terribly much at ease where I am, in my body, in my house, in my landscape, in my community." This confidence imbues Hall's current writing. *Seasons at Eagle Pond* (1987), written with a lyricism reminiscent of Thoreau, uses the cycle of the seasons as a symbolic bridge to unite past and present. During the moderate winter of 1987, Hall merges his own memory with that of his ancestors to call up the blizzard of 1888 and restore ties to a world otherwise lost in time. A similar impulse shapes Hall's verse play, *The Bone Ring* (1987), which adapts for the stage an earlier volume of childhood recollections, *String Too Short to Be Saved* (1961; rev. ed. 1979). Rich with Hall's intricate sense of local tradition, the play features characters from four generations whose shared memories stretch back to the surrender at Appomattox. Another book, *The Ideal Bakery* (1987), transposes Hall's complex amalgam of past and present into the genre of the short story.

But Hall is first of all a poet, and the plenitude of his mature vision is especially evident in the poems he has written since his retirement to New Hampshire. A note of repose is sounded in the later pieces of *Kicking the Leaves* (1978) and then extended in his most recent books, *The Happy Man* (1986) and *The One Day* (1988). This repose is, however, strikingly unsentimental, everywhere beset by contingency and loss. But although pain is carefully registered, Hall finally enfolds it into the larger rhythms of nature and history.

This ability to resolve emotional conflict marks no sudden turn in Hall's work but grows steadily out of long obedience to poetry's power to reveal the self. The process began in 1957 when Hall realized that the rational and technical rigors he had imposed on his early verse were, in fact, repressive devices, motivated by a personal "fear of inspiration, a fear of the imagination, a fear of the loss of control." At that moment Hall committed himself to a "poetry of spiritual freedom" that gives voice to the "dream self" and proceeds more by improvisation than intellection. "In recent years," he explains, "I have come to accept the beginning of a poem, or even a whole draft, without the slightest clue to the subject matter."

The search for poetic forms responsive to the self's deepest demands has carried Hall through many changes in the years since 1957, but the quest had not yet started when at age twenty-five he wrote "My Son, My Executioner" at Stanford. Looking back on the poem more than twenty years later, Hall remarked: "Meter, rhyme, paradox, irony, abstraction. I no longer quite know the person who wrote this poem, though I remember him dimly, as if recalling not a person but a photograph." But the piece was one of the boldest achievements of *Exiles and Marriages,* and it is still the most often anthologized of Hall's works.

In 1953-4, I dropped by Yvor Winters' office, where we held our tiny poetry workshop twice a week, ten or fifteen minutes before class. Winters sat at his desk, smoking his pipe as he read. Perhaps he sighed as he closed his book, but then we talked, mostly about poetry: prosody, Ben Jonson, "Homage to Mistress Bradstreet" in the new *Partisan*. Also we joked or teased, especially about New England and California. Winters might say, poker-faced, "Yes, I know that New England landscape: flat, a few rivers wandering through. I know it well; I spent a whole summer in Gambier, Ohio." While I flapped in outrage he would giggle and his great stomach shake.

One day he was reading Hart Crane as I entered, and he grumbled about Crane's ideas and about "Professor X" again. That day I said, "Why do you read him, then?" It was a real question. He paused a moment and without expression said, "Because he's so beautiful."

That year I took no classes except for the workshop, but Winters sensibly asked fellowship students to audit one of his literature classes each term, where we could observe his ideas in the sites they derived from. The first course I audited was the most devastating; I think it was "The Theory and Practice of the Criticism of Poetry" but it could have been "The Systematic Annihilation of the Collected Poems of G.M. Hopkins and W.B. Yeats." I let him have Hopkins because I didn't know enough to argue but I didn't let him have Yeats, the love of my life at that time; of course, Winters *took* him anyway: I never won an argument. After he had destroyed a Yeats poem he would turn to me: "And what does Mr. Hall have to say?" When I tried out some contradiction he would rip my arguments and scatter them on the floor. He was not cruel; the exercise was instructive; although always defeated I was not always convinced.

When we brought a poem to workshop, he would glance through it, read it aloud, and then deliver a small essay about it--the quickest study I have ever witnessed. What remains with me is not so much his judgment of poems as certain practical principles by which he judged. I gathered notions about diction (notably dead metaphor) and about prosody (Jespersen and relative stress) that become stronger as I become older.

That year I wrote a poem on the birth of my son Andrew, quatrains which I now call "My Son, My Executioner." Winters approved of it, relatively; he *nodded*, I think, in a gratifying manner. It took me ten years to decide to leave off the fourth stanza, but I think I was finally right. The fourth stanza was redundant; it dug its elbow in the reader's ribs: "In case you didn't get it, this is what I just told you." In addition, it irredeemably rhymed breath and death.

Donald Hall

Selected Works by Donald Hall

Poetry

Exiles and Marriages. New York: Viking, 1955.
The Alligator Bride: Poems New and Selected. New York: Harper & Row, 1969.
The Town of Hill. Boston: Godine, 1975.
Kicking the Leaves. New York: Harper & Row, 1978.
The Toy Bone. Brockport: Boa, 1979.
The Happy Man. New York: Random House, 1986.
The One Day. New York: Ticknor & Fields, 1988.

Fiction

The Ideal Bakery. Berkeley: North Point Press, 1987.

Other

String Too Short to Be Saved. New York: Viking, 1961.
Henry Moore: The Life and Work of a Great Sculptor. New York: Harper & Row, 1966.
Marianne Moore: The Cage and the Animal. New York: Pegasus, 1970.
As the Eye Moves: A Sculpture by Henry Moore. New York: Abrams, 1970.
Writing Well. Boston: Little Brown, 1973; revised editions, 1976, 1979.
Dock Ellis in the Country of Baseball, with Dock Ellis. New York: Coward McCann, 1976.
Remembering Poets: Reminiscences and Opinions--Dylan Thomas, Robert Frost, T.S. Eliot, Ezra Pound. New York: Harper & Row, 1978.
Goatfoot Milktongue Twinbird: Interviews, Essays, Notes on Poetry 1970-76. Ann Arbor: University of Michigan Press, 1978.

Ox-Cart Man (for children). New York: Viking, 1979.
To Keep Moving. Geneva, New York: Seneca, 1980.
The Weather of Poetry: Essays Reviews, and Notes on Poetry 1977-81. Ann Arbor: University of Michigan Press, 1982.
The Man Who Lived Alone (for children). Boston: Godine, 1984.
Fathers Playing Catch with Sons: Essays on Sport. Berkeley: North Point Press, 1985.
Seasons at Eagle Pond. New York: Ticknor & Fields, 1987.
The Bone Ring. Santa Cruz: Story Line, 1987.
Poetry and Ambition: Essays 1982-88. Ann Arbor: University of Michigan Press, 1988.

Editor, *New Poets of England and America.* Cleveland: Meridian, 1957; *Second Selection,* 1962.
Editor, *Contemporary American Poetry.* Harmondsworth: Penguin, 1962; revised edition, 1971.
Editor, *The Faber Book of Modern Verse,* revised edition. London: Faber, 1965.
Editor, *The Pleasures of Poetry.* New York: Harper & Row, 1971.
Editor, *The Oxford Book of American Literary Anecdotes.* New York: Oxford University Press, 1981.
Editor, *The Oxford Book of Children's Verse in America.* New York: Oxford University Press, 1985.

Donald Hall's son, Andrew, was born in the spring of 1954 when Hall was twenty-five years old and studying poetry with Yvor Winters at Stanford. Even while celebrating the birth of his child, says Hall, "I had the sense of his replacing me and therefore, of my own necessary death." These simultaneous feelings of love and mortality inspired the poem, "My Son, My Executioner," which appeared in the New Yorker *later that same year, and was then collected as "Epigenethlion: First Child" in Hall's first major book of poetry,* Exiles and Marriages *(1955).*

More than a decade later, Andrew, now nearly fourteen, gave Hall new insight into the poem's emotional origins, when he said: "That poem you wrote about me when I was born, that's really about you and your daddy, isn't it?" At that point Hall realized "My Son, My Executioner" is "much more a memory of my feelings toward my own father than it is, actually, about me and my baby son. Having a baby son apparently reminded me of the feelings toward the father which every man must have, the wish to take the father's place." The poem's energy, Hall comments, "comes from the conflict of desire and guilt over desire."

1.

2.

1. "I have never written a poem in one draft," Hall says, and he rewrote "My Son, My Executioner" repeatedly in the months that followed his son's birth. In this first manuscript draft, the original version of the opening stanza is immediately revised, with the poem's first line, "My son, my executioner," now used as a refrain for the piece as a whole.

At this point, the poem is in four stanzas, the final one written vertically in the upper right-hand margin. Although Hall ultimately kept much of the language of the third and fourth stanzas, the second was unsatisfactory. Here he crosses it out and in subsequent drafts will change it almost entirely. Interestingly, only in this first manuscript does Hall address his son by name.

2. After several revisions Hall expanded the poem to five stanzas and added a title, here inserted in the upper left-hand margin. "Epigenethlion" is a Greek derivative that literally means "upon a birth." Hall took the title from another poetry student in Winters's class, who had used it on his own verses for Andrew's birth. When the New Yorker printed the poem, Hall followed the editor's suggestion and changed the title to "First Child." When republished in Exiles and Marriages, the poem carried a combination of the two earlier titles, "Epigenethlion: First Child."

Not until it appeared in The Alligator Bride (1968) did Hall call it "My Son, My Executioner."

An important feature of this draft is Hall's careful circling of those words and lines that he will later rewrite. In addition, Hall also revises directly. The most significant changes occur in the second stanza, where he emends the description of his child as "the testament/Of immortality" to "the testment/Of our mortality" and in the last stanza, where "The earthly paradox" becomes "The mortal paradox." These revisions capture Hall's mixed feelings about fatherhood and emphasize the irony at the poem's center--that the child is both a guarantee of Hall's existence in the future and the seal of his impending death.

3.

EPIGENETHLION

My son, my executioner,
    I take you in my arms,
Quiet and small and just astir,
    And whom my body warms,
        My son, my executioner.

Sweet death, small son, our instrument
    Of immortality,
~~We in your presence are content~~   Your cries & hungers document
    ~~With~~ bodily decay,   Our
        My son, my executioner.

We twenty-five and twenty-two,
    Who seemed to live forever,
Observe enduring life in you,
    And start to die together,
        My son, my executioner.

I take into my arms the death
    Maturity exacts,
And ~~praise~~ with my imperfect breath
    The mortal paradox,
        My son, my executioner.

4.

3. In the next manuscript, Hall reworks the elements he had circled on the earlier draft and also decides to delete entirely the third stanza. Noteworthy as well is his revision of the fourth stanza. By changing the preceding draft's phrase, "Observe our bodies' end in you," to "Observe surviving life in you," Hall subtly redirects the line's thematic emphasis from mortality to immortality. This exactly counterbalances the changes he had just made in the previous draft. The effect is to intensify the ambiguity of Hall's feelings about fatherhood.

At the level of formal technique, Hall's method for choosing among rhyme words is clearly illustrated in the lower right-hand margin, where he lists a wide variety of possibilties before selecting the option most appropriate for both sound and sense.

4. In this first typescript Hall makes local changes that bring the poem closer to the state in which it appeared in the New Yorker. There is, however, one major revision still to occur that is not evident here-- Hall's decision to eliminate the refrain. This move, perhaps the boldest in the poem's composition, is typical of Hall, who revises mainly by deletions, sometimes quite drastic and dramatic. Hall is acutely conscious of the reason: "I tend to explain too much. I tend to go into too much detail," and as a consequence, he adds,"it takes me a long time to come to the clarity and intensity of the single thrust of the feeling." By eliminating the hammering repetitions of "My son, my executioner," Hall broke the grip of overstatement and released the poem's paradoxical emotions from the refrain's thematic simplicity.

Hall's process of deletion did not end for several years. Even after the poem's initial success, he remained unhappy with the fourth stanza's overstatement and, he explains, "at some point in the 1960s I learned enough to suppress [it]." Consequently, when the poem appeared again in his 1968 collection of new and selected verse, The Alligator Bride, only the first three stanzas remained. Although "My Son, My Executioner" has continued to grow shorter over the years, its power has intensified with each cut.

Robert Hass

"Survival is the art around here," Robert Hass remarks in *Praise* (1979), his second book of poems. This line—direct, colloquial, serious without portentousness—catches the dominant tone of Hass's eclectic career as poet, critic, editor, and translator. The survival in question is of the self and personal desire amid what Hass regards as the century's catastrophic "redundancy of violence and suffering." Of all the contemporary tools for emotional survival, Hass is most deeply sympathetic to modernist literature and its techniques for securing the self against the devastations of history. He celebrates the power of aesthetic form to heal "our experience of fragmentation," and he eloquently endorses the modernist assumption that "being human" means "to be constantly making one's place in language, in consciousness, in imagination." But in the battle to keep the self alive and desire quick, Hass also knows that "There are limits to imagination." Indeed, for him, it is not imagination but life's commonplace events that empower art. This profound ambivalence about the aesthetics of modernism lies at the very heart of Hass's performance, prompting him both to appropriate and to subvert its methods. The result is a subtle revision of literary strategy that offers a distinctly new stance in the fight to stay passionately alert to our world.

A native Californian, Hass was born in San Francisco in 1941 and grew up in the Bay Area. After completing his undergraduate studies at St. Mary's College in Moraga, he came to Stanford in 1963 to pursue a doctorate in English, which he received in 1971 with the submission of his dissertation on economic ideology in the classical novel. While at Stanford, Hass was an active member of the poetic community, though he never formally enrolled in Yvor Winters's workshops and deliberately remained outside Winters's circle. During these years he began taking his poetry seriously, particularly, Hass explains, after "I found out that I could write about myself and the world I knew, San Francisco and the country around it, in a fairly simple and direct way." In 1967, while still at work on his dissertation, he accepted an appointment to the faculty of the State University of New York at Buffalo. Hass stayed in Buffalo until 1971, then returned to the West Coast to continue his academic career at St. Mary's. By that time, his poems were regularly appearing in national magazines, and he had been included in Paul Carroll's important anthology, *The Younger American Poets* (1968). Today Hass still teaches at his alma mater, though over the years he has also been a poet-in-residence and visiting lecturer at numerous other schools, including the University of Virginia, Columbia University, and the University of California at Berkeley.

Hass's first collection of poetry, *Field Guide* (1973), was chosen by Stanley Kunitz for the Yale Series of Younger Poets Award. Its opening section, "The Coast," and its closing section, "In Weather," are centered geographically, drawing their topics from Hass's experiences in California and Buffalo respectively, while the middle section focuses self-consciously on writers and writing, directly addressing art's relation to life. The book's title signals the characteristic movement of Hass's verse. A field guide, like poetry itself, is a highly conventionalized genre, with its own internal logic and stylized methods of description; also like poetry, it prizes clarity of language and precision of images. But unlike modernist literature, a field guide insists on reaching beyond its own artifice, deliberately directing its users to the world outside the text. It is at just this intersection of the aesthetic and the actual that Hass situates his own art. His poems are exquisitely crafted pieces whose rhythms hypnotize attention, but at the same moment, the lucidity of their language dissolves toward transparency and pushes the reader outside the poem into the "literal insistences" of the world.

Typical of Hass's complex dialectic is "Letter," which concerns desire and the limits of literature. Addressed to his absent wife, the poem begins by confidently asserting Hass's ability to recover through his imagination the pleasures he takes in his family. "I have believed so long/in the magic of names and poems," Hass says, "I hadn't thought them bodiless/at all." But as his imagination falters, he begins to doubt language's power to contain what he loves. "It all seemed real to me/last week. Words." As Hass increasingly fears art's inadequacy to satisfy his longing, the poem reaches a crisis and abruptly abandons the modernist mystique of language. "You are the body/of my world, root and flower," Hass says emphatically to his wife, concluding, "you're the names of things." This reversal of the conventional relation between words and referents beautifully displaces literature with life. But Hass's elevation of the literal is paradoxically achieved through the magic of his poetic language—a complex gesture that celebrates the imagination it otherwise forsakes.

Hass continues to develop this masterfully ambivalent style of modernism in *Praise*, which received the William Carlos Williams Award in 1979. The collection draws on an especially broad range of historical and cultural references. "Against Botticelli," for example, adopts elements of art history to examine the threats to vitality posed by aesthetic form, while "Meditation at Lagunitas" invokes the concepts of French deconstructive thought to express Hass's abiding suspicion that "a word is elegy to what it signifies." Though intellectually demanding, the poems in *Praise* are completely accessible, perhaps nowhere more poignantly so than in "Songs to Survive the Summer," the extended meditative lyric that concludes the book. Addressed to his daughter, it anecdotally rehearses the consolations of science, literature, and religion, exposing the limits of each in turn and finally coming to rest in a moving catalog of inconsequential particulars that forms his legacy: "That is what I have/to give you, child, stories,/songs, loquat seeds,/curiously shaped; they/are the frailest stay against/our fears."

The modesty, generosity, and emotional intimacy so evident in Hass's poetry also characterize his criticism, much of which is gathered in *Twentieth Century Pleasures* (1984). Stylistically, his prose is distinguished by a clarity of thought that handles difficult concepts with stunning ease, and by the powerful presence of autobiography. These two elements combine to create a uniquely personalized medium that Hass uses to reshape our understanding of twentieth-century literature. At the thematic level, there is a double movement to Hass's project. On the one hand, he offers a series of sensitive but ultimately reserved appreciations of such American modernist writers as Yvor Winters, Robert Lowell, Robert Creeley, and Robinson Jeffers, an important selection of whose poetry Hass has also edited. On the other hand, he reaches outside his native literary tradition to both European and Oriental masters, including Rainer Maria Rilke, Tomas Tranströmer, Czeslaw Milosz, Yosa Buson, and Basho. Hass's interest in these foreign voices is closely connected to his reservations about American modernism, which center on its willful ignorance of history and its innocent faith in art's power. "I wanted to read a poetry by people who did not assume that the great drama in their work was that everything in the world was happening to them for the first time," Hass comments in explaining his attraction to foreign writers. To introduce his American audience to their very different perspectives, Hass has not only written important essays on them but also edited a collection of Tranströmer and translated two of Milosz's books, one in collaboration with Robert Pinsky. In alliance with his quietly subversive poetry, Hass's work as critic and translator opens another front in the redirection of American literature toward a more humane engagement with the contemporary world.

My memories of the writing scene at Stanford—I arrived in the fall of 1963—begin with Yvor Winters in the classroom. I took his large lecture course on English poetry and I remember his coming in the first day of class, his vinous, somehow watery aspect, and his manner, somber, perhaps theatrically weary. He wore a suit cut in the roomy style of the late 1940's, and a black armband, in mourning, we heard, for the four black children killed that summer in the bombing of a Birmingham church that was attempting to register voters. He kept it on to mourn the murder of John Kennedy in November. It was the beginning of a violent time. Through it Winters lectured—his manner toward us students involved an impatience or show of impatience that amounted to contempt—with singleminded ferocity and passion about poetry as an art supremely able to register with precision and understanding the shocks of human experience.

It was an amazing performance, and I was both dazzled and appalled by it. I decided not to study with him. He was much too powerful and singular a presence for someone as unformed as I was, and the kind of restraint and sobriety he recommended to young poets and praised in his various disciples had to me at twenty-one the look of a superannuation derby. I was unsure about whether I could write poems at all, but it was the gift of listening to Winters talk that he made it seem the thing most worth doing. I spent some years arguing with him in my head, instead of signing up for his workshop.

In fact, one of the reasons I got involved in the creation of—as we said in those days—the free university was to start a counter-workshop, which we did, John Peck and I. John was an admiring drop-out from Winters' seminar and we did get a group going which traded poems and read and studied poets outside the Winters canon.

Stanford was very lively at that time and it was full of young poets, a fact commemorated by a book called *Five American Poets* and published by the Carcanet Press in England. The five were Peck, me, Robert Pinsky, Jim McMichael, and John Matthias, all at Stanford at that time. Ken Fields, of course, was also there. And there were others, particularly Sharon Olds, then Sharon Cobb, whom I knew generically as one of the undergraduates who hung out at the *Sequoia* office. It was not until later, in New York, after I had read *The Dead and the Living* and *The Gold Cell*, that we became friends and realized that we had come out of that same moment.

Albert Guerard was a very generous presence for young writers. He had brought John Hawkes to the campus to run an experiment in the teaching of writing called the Voice Project. Hawkes had brought with him a group of young novelists, Jerome Charyn, Mark Mirsky, Jay Neugeboren, all still quite active, and the crucial person for me, the poet and novelist Mitchell Goodman, who was then married to Denise Levertov. I was terrifically interested in her work, and through Mitch she came to read at just about the time—1964? '65?—when she was beginning to write about Vietnam; the reading brought with it a sense of windows being opened, of new energy in the art. (I also remember a dinner before the reading at Jack Hawkes' house. I was mute, slightly awed, the youngest member of the company, and listened while Hawkes spoke of how much he loved Denise's poem, "Scenes from the Life of Pepper Trees," how he loved the very idea of pepper trees, even though he never expected to see anything so exotic. I busily revised my idea of the alertness of artists, since the main feature of his Menlo Park house was a huge pepper tree in the front yard.)

That summer Donald Davie came to visit for the first time and taught a summer course in contemporary American poets. We read the work of Gary Snyder, William Stafford, Sylvia Plath, Ed Dorn. The work of Snyder and Dorn could only be found then in small press chapbooks, which Davie had located. We read them closely. He is in many ways temperamentally akin to Winters, so it was fascinating to watch his exacting intelligence and fastidious ear at work on what then seemed the experimental tradition in American writing.

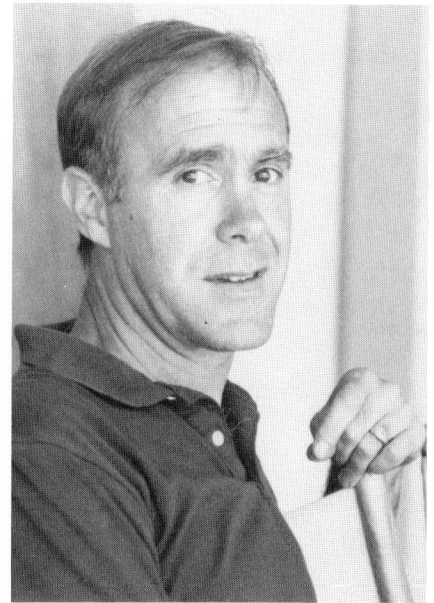

Several of us were also involved in political activities stimulated by the Free Speech Movement (not sure it needs to be capitalized) in Berkeley. Through them I got to know Peck and Pinsky a little. I had begun to edit a newsletter to print research that some of us had been doing on the war-related contracts at Stanford Research Institute, then a mysterious entity. We called the first issue the *Graduate Coordinating Committee Newsletter*, which sounded to us like serious business. By the third issue it had become a newspaper with a name, *Commitment: A Journal of the Asylum*, and a penchant for throwing large parties to which one wore utopian light blue J.C. Penney work-shirts, the unofficial uniform of the Student Non-Violent Coordinating Committee, and at which one saw for the first time the black corduroy Greek fishermen's caps made popular by the head of Bob Dylan as pho-tographed on the cover of his second or third album. That was the ambi-ence. Hair was getting longer. Once there was a newspaper, it needed to be filled, and I began to fill it with poems—Peck's, Pinsky's, mine. I even printed some poems under pseudonyms when I had gaping holes to fill and didn't want to look like a vanity press. Peck and I collaborated on essays on some of the poets we read in Davie's class, and we printed those too.

And there were a couple of pieces —another complex bit of Stanford history—by Dennis Sweeney, who was something of a campus hero. He had been in Mississippi—as one might say now that someone did political organizing in Soweto—and wrote first-hand reports of it, and many years later he played out a dra-ma begun in Palo Alto by murdering his Stanford mentor Allard Lowenstein, then a New York con-gressman, whom Dennis in a state of psychotic paranoia believed to be a CIA agent tormenting him by having radio signals transmitted to the fill-ings in his teeth. In 1965 or so Dennis was a clear-eyed young man in jeans and a workshirt who carried around a copy of Camus' *The Rebel* and Al Lowenstein was any young Stanford dean in a tweed jacket and horn-rimmed glasses.

The more resolutely political of the editors of the paper disliked all the literary stuff and they eventually changed the name of the paper to *Resistance*. It lasted under that more adamant masthead for several years, until about the time that the faculty voted to expel Bruce Franklin, a pro-fessor of English, from their ranks for his part in a demonstration against the military research at SRI. By then

most of the 55,000 Americans who died in Vietnam were dead, and the poets of my generation had moved on.

It should be said that in the mid-dle of all this we were studying English literature—I remember sitting in the back of Albert Guerard's Wordsworth class with Pinsky and, one of the more solid pleasures of graduate work, making fun of the oral reports, as they were called, delivered dutifully or feverishly or with an air of doomed improvisation by the other students. And we were beginning families. It was fairly unusual for graduate students to be married, but Peck, Pinsky, McMichael, and I—I don't know what it was about us—were all married. I remem-ber walking in the Palo Alto marshes early on Saturday mornings with my young son, looking at birds, teaching myself the marsh grasses, and begin-ning to try to hum out to myself the lines of poems that eventually appeared in my first book, *Field Guide*.

Robert Hass

Selected Works by Robert Hass

Poetry

Field Guide. New Haven: Yale University Press, 1973.
Praise. New York: Ecco Press, 1979.
Human Wishes. New York: Ecco Press, 1989.

Other

Twentieth Century Pleasures. New York: Ecco Press, 1984.

Editor, *Rock and Hawk: A Selection of Shorter Verse by Robinson Jeffers.* New York: Random House, 1987.
Editor, *Tomas Tranströmer: Selected Poems, 1954-1986.* New York: Ecco Press, 1987.

Translator, with Robert Pinsky, *The Separate Notebooks,* by Czeslaw Milosz. New York: Ecco Press, 1984.
Translator, *Unattainable Earth,* by Czeslaw Milosz. New York: Ecco Press, 1986.

1.

1: During his years at Stanford as a doctoral student in English, Robert Hass kept notebooks which he used not only for course-related materials but also for drafts of his poetry. Sometimes the manuscript versions of poems that appear in the notebooks are virtually identical to their later published forms. Typical of this pattern is "On the Coast near Sausalito," which recounts Hass's catching a cabezone on a fishing expedition. On the page of the notebook preceding the text, Hass copies information about the fish that he gathered from library research. Hardly any of these descriptive terms are, however, carried over into the draft. The poem first appeared in a 1967 number of Hudson Review and was later collected, without further revisions, in Hass's first book, Field Guide (1973).

2. "Palo Alto: The Marshes," also a poem Hass wrote at Stanford, published in the Hudson Review, and later collected in Field Guide, shows a more complex evolution in another of his student notebooks. The poem is initially titled "Mariana Richardson" and its tentative beginning is sandwiched between miscellaneous definitions, word lists, and fragments of other poems. After two stanzas, Hass breaks off this draft to record a paragraph of biographical information about the nineteenth-century Hispanic woman whose life enables the poem to take the moral measure of contemporary California. The next manuscript version follows immediately in the notebook and marks a major advance in Hass's conception of the poem. Now titled "For Mariana Richardson (1832-1903)," it is divided into eleven separately numbered sections. Parts 1, 2, and 4 already approximate their printed versions, but most of the other segments are rough sketches or mere indications of topics at this point. On the notebook's next page, Hass considers a different concluding sequence. He follows section 11 with outlines for four new sections and an unspecified sixteenth, clearly indicating that he had not yet fixed the poem's final structure. Eventually Hass renamed the poem and limited it to eleven sections.

2a.

2b.

Donald Justice

When Donald Justice's *Selected Poems* received the Pulitzer Prize in 1980, American letters honored a writer of exceptional achievement. For four decades Justice has pursued an unfashionably conservative aesthetic, but with an originality so radical that his poetry opens new possibilities for traditionalist verse. For him, artistic form is not an organic extension of content that mimics the contingencies of everyday experience. It is, rather, an abstract pattern similar to musical structure, endowed with an order and clarity free from the confusions of life. Though Justice insists on form's independence from content, he sees it as neither arbitrary nor empty but powerfully expressive, capable of intimating rhythms of feeling and thought that are beyond language's semantic threshold.

Justice's first book, *The Summer Anniversaries* (1960), demonstrates his mastery of a wide range of traditional poetic forms. The volume includes sonnets, sestinas, and odes as well as variations on the villanelle—all handled with a finesse that both respects literary conventions and subtly alters their rules to extend the limits of each form. This technical virtuosity is one of the pleasures of Justice's poetry. "There's something of the game" in these elaborately artificial forms, he explains, a game that "has no end beyond itself—virtually the definition of the esthetic." But form also serves another purpose in *The Summer Anniversaries*. Many of its poems are about loss—of youth and beauty, of friends and family, of love and sanity—and form is Justice's means for salvaging fragments of that wholeness which now lives only in memory. "One of the motives for writing," he says, "is surely to recover and hold what would otherwise be lost totally. . .so that one might not wholly die."

Several of the poems in *Summer Anniversaries* recall Justice's Southern childhood. Born in 1925, he grew up in Miami, which he describes as a "sleepy, middle-sized Southern city" during these Depression years. His father was a carpenter and the family, with roots reaching back to Georgia and Alabama, was poor. Though he read a lot as a child and wrote both poems and stories in adolescence, Justice's first love was not literature but music. His piano lessons were one of the emotional centers of his life, and he struggled hard to teach himself musical composition. Not until he was an undergraduate at the University of Miami did Justice finally receive his first professional instruction from the composer Carl Ruggles, but by then the moment for a career in music had passed. And so, after completing his undergraduate studies, Justice took an M. A. in English at the University of North Carolina. Then in 1948 he came to Stanford, intending to pursue his doctorate. Justice had already published his first poems in national literary magazines, and he supplemented his required courses in English by attending Yvor Winters's classes in poetry. After a year at Stanford, he realized that he cared less about the academic profession of literature than about creative writing, and he decided to leave the program. When Justice did receive his Ph.D., in 1954, it was from the Writers Workshop at the University of Iowa, where he studied under John Berryman, Robert Lowell, and Karl Shapiro, submitting a group of his own poems for his dissertation. By the time *The Summer Anniversaries* appeared in 1960, Justice had returned to Iowa as a member of the Workshop's faculty. That appointment he kept until 1982, except for a period during the late 1960s and early 1970s, when he taught at Syracuse University. Today he teaches in his native state at the University of Florida.

A scrupulous craftsman who has always worked slowly, Justice did not publish his second collection of poems until 1967. When *Night Light* appeared, he had already entered his forties, and—as the title suggests—a subdued, self-consciously middle-aged mood informs much of the volume. Though more somber than *The Summer Anniversaries*, this new collection sustains the concerns of the first book. Formally, Justice continues to develop original variations on the traditional repertoire of meters and stanzas, but he also extends his range into loose syllabic and free verse patterns. Justice's command of both closed and open forms is unusual. In fact, many poets consider the two modes to represent conflicting cultural ideologies. But for Justice, the differences are more technical than moral, their complementary values residing in the rhythmic subtleties each alone can render.

Thematically, life's mutability and memory's power to arrest the steady erosion of experience remain Justice's focus in *Night Light*. The springs of his sense of loss vary widely. Some are predictable—the prospect of old age, the suicides of friends, war's outrages. Others are poignantly incidental—a hatbox of old letters listed in a newspaper advertisement, a dressmaker's dummy, an abandoned line of verse. But in every instance, what finally compels attention is less the poem's content than a distinctive movement of consciousness delicately caught in the formal play of Justice's lines. As these abstract patterns of perception and feeling haunt our thoughts, we understand that they transcend the particularities of experience, and we recognize in them the psychological warp on which the fabric of all our lives is woven.

In his next book, *Departures* (1973), Justice again seeks new formal means to capture the musical essence of a world rapidly receding from our grasp. This ambition is especially evident in his invention of the poetic sonatina, which began for Justice as a challenge of finding in grammar and syntax the equivalent of a musical structure. But as he worked at this technical problem in "Sonatina in Yellow" and "Sonatina in Green," form once more declared its affinity with memory and became a vehicle for conveying art's power to evoke and preserve the past.

Departures also offers other new forms, including poems produced from verbal games and riddles as well as one generated by chance. It was, in fact, the death of Robert Kennedy that provoked Justice to adopt aleatoric techniques when he composed "The Assasination." Though deeply upset by the murder, he did not want the poem to be a vehicle for his own moral and political outrage. "I don't like to think of myself," Justice insists, "as a propagandist or an evangelist." To avoid speaking in a vatic voice, Justice relied on an impersonal mechanism to organize the poem. Compiling separate decks of cards for nouns, verbs, adjectives, and syntax patterns, Justice shuffled each and then dealt himself sentences. This maneuver released him from the grip of immediate feelings and pushed his attention away from social issues into aesthetic concerns. The result is a poem that deftly transfigures emotional shock into rhythms of such beautiful urgency that they linger in the mind long after the event's specific details have receded.

The conjunction of music and memory also animates much of *The Sunset Maker* (1987), Justice's most recent book. His first collection since revising his earlier work for *Selected Poems*, the volume extends Justice's formal innovations beyond the boundaries of verse. In one sequence, he transposes the same theme from metered sonnet through prose memoir and then into free verse meditation. As the subtle differences between these keys resonate, we realize Justice has discovered another dimension of language's ability to sound even the quietest accents of our evanescent world.

Yvor Winters was an early hero of mine. *In Defense of Reason,* at the time newly published, was a wedding present, and I read it on my honeymoon. Like several of my "modernist" friends, I already knew *Primativism and Decadence* and *Maule's Curse* pretty thoroughly. It was possible in the mid-forties to regard Winters as a radical theorist on literary matters, as we did; and though I would argue that it is still possible to do so, the case is too long to make here.

So it was in its way inevitable that in the late summer of 1948 my considerate wife and I found ourselves on a bus heading from North Carolina for Palo Alto, where I intended to study with Winters. A friend from Chapel Hill, Edgar Bowers, had already pioneered this cross-country route. The very first poem Edgar had sent back from Stanford—"Epigram on the Passing of Christmas"—convinced me to follow. This poem was a good deal beyond anything he had done at Chapel Hill, clear, metrically firm, confident, expressive. In its small way—it is only four lines long—it seemed a revelation to me then, and it must have seemed so to Edgar as well, perhaps even to Winters himself. Over the next couple of years Edgar was to write a series of astonishing poems, not nearly as well known still as they ought to be, except perhaps by Wintersians; and it was to become one of the great pleasures of my year at Stanford to be shown poems like his "Grove and Building" or "The Mountain Cemetery" within days of their completion.

I was a Ph.D. student and teaching assistant with a heavy load, and the policy of the chairman would not allow me to enroll in Winters' classes for credit, a bitter disappointment. But very generously Winters gave me permission to visit his classes when I could manage, though I was never to become a member of the inner circle. From him I think I learned as much as from any other teacher ever, which was still not as much as in my hero-worshipping innocence I could have hoped for. I did learn the meters, for which I have always been grateful. Nor did I fail to profit in unforeseeable ways from what was even then his defiantly idiosyncratic but always honorable and hard-headed approach to literature and to teaching. It was enough to turn me a little aside toward fiction, which I had always loved anyhow. But this was a secret love and did not take even the outward form of visits to the classes in fiction, not more than once or twice anyhow, and then quietly. I read *Middlemarch, Anna Karenina,* a lot of Conrad, and in magazines the new Welty stories that were to make up *The Golden Apples;* no year since has matched that one for great fiction.

And then one day, crossing Middlefield Road, I had for one of the few times in my life something like an actual inspiration. In a flash of vision a scene came to me from nowhere; at least it did not in any recognizable way come from experience. The story I wrote to work up to that scene naturally enough failed to live up to the vision itself, but it did win second prize in that year's short story contest. This prize was providential. The $150 prize money paid our train fare back to Miami, where I had a job teaching. So came about my escape from a graduate school in which I had not been given much of a chance to study what I wanted and needed. The progress allowed—one course a quarter, when I could easily have handled two or three—was so agonizingly slow that even now at times I fantasize myself still plugging away endlessly at the ever-receding degree. What a year it had been, all the same! And no doubt the decades would have rolled by as pleasantly as that one year had done, all eucalyptus and mild sunshine and yellow jackets buzzing our coffee cups in the patio—but I could not afford the time.

Donald Justice

Selected Works by Donald Justice

Poetry

The Summer Anniversaries. Middletown: Wesleyan University Press, 1960.
Night Light. Middletown: Wesleyan University Press, 1967.
Departures. New York: Atheneum, 1973.
Selected Poems. New York: Atheneum, 1979.
The Sunset Maker. New York: Atheneum, 1987.

Other

Platonic Scripts (includes interviews). Ann Arbor: University of Michigan Press, 1984.

Editor, *The Collected Poems of Weldon Kees.* Iowa City: Stone Wall Press, 1960; revised edition, Lincoln: University of Nebraska Press, 1975.
Editor, *Contemporary French Poetry.* Ann Arbor: University of Michigan Press, 1965.

Donald Justice comments: "Here are three manuscript pages from work published in *The Sunset Maker* (1987). One represents the second or third draft of a passage near the end of a short story, 'Little Elegy for Cello and Piano.' One is the first draft of the title poem in the book, which I made from the short story; and the last is a very late revision of the same poem, done on a Xerox of the text as it appeared in a magazine.

"They show, all these years later, the double pull of fiction and poetry which that year at Stanford seemed to foreshadow, though in fact, to my regret, I have written very few stories.

"In this case the story came first. Like the Stanford story it arrived by way of a moment of 'inspiration'—a recital one Sunday afternoon at the Phillips Collection in Washington, when, as a consequence of somebody's sneeze, I realized that certain notes had been lost to me forever. Two years passed before I had the idea of trying to put the end of the story into blank verse—not, I am well aware, a blank verse that would have met altogether with Winters's approval, since for his taste it has, among other things, an unusually high proportion of extra light syllables. The composer is modeled upon another early teacher of mine, Carl Ruggles, and the musical phrase is half of a tone row recalled from a quartet written at age seventeen for Ruggles. The whole phrase, for anyone curious, went like this:

So it is not yet quite lost, not altogether."

1. "I happen to be a constant reviser," Justice says, and the handwritten notations packed densely on this typescript of "Little Elegy for Cello and Piano" bear colorful witness to his statement. Red, blue, green, and black inks indicate different layers of revision; the last pass, in black, includes Justice's careful totalling of the number of words on the rewritten page.

Most of the changes in the first two paragraphs involve subtle variations of phrase, reflecting Justice's impeccable ear. In contrast, Justice signals a major thematic shift by referring to the French painter Pierre Bonnard in his manuscript additions to the third paragraph. In the typescript, he imagines Bestor's music surviving in nature through a scientifically conceived "eternity of sounds." The allusion to Bonnard redirects attention to human memory and its ability to preserve the past through art.

Little Elegy - p. 7 (3-23)

The manuscripts have come down to me. One day, I suppose, the library of the college in Vermont will take them. Meanwhile, I take out the pages of Eugene's last composition and let my eye run over the calligraphy of the notes, climbing the staves, lingeringly dwellingly, there hovering like clouds, entire flocks of birds above the top line. But it is all a little beyond my present skills. I pick out the notes of the piano part, but it is not the same. In any case, I have not heard of a cellist in all the extent of this new sun-and-sand community to which I have retired. Perhaps there is one in the nearest junior college, but that is miles and miles away, across a causeway,

I sit back and listen to the surf. I cannot see it but I can hear it. The sun is just easing its way down, scattering color. The truth is, I can hear it much better now than at the keyboard. I wonder how many others who were present in the Phillips that afternoon can still summon up any of what by now must surely be the broken web of sounds heard then, as I can, partially and just barely. The last three plucked chords--surely they resonate for still, though fading. And soon remember how any of it sounded at all.

Yet I cannot doubt that there does exist a sort of eternity of sounds, somewhere, let us say, in the atmosphere. Surely there are scientific grounds to believe this. And in this eternity of sounds the beautiful, delicate notes of persevere. They endure, energy--pure energy of the pure spirit and are not lost. I cannot hear them but they are there. Like the surf.

(Sunday??)

SMALL ELEGY FOR CELLO & PIANO recital
— After a performance at the Phillips Collection

The Bestor manuscripts have come ~~down~~ to me.   ~~came~~
And I, in my turn, ~~shall~~ will bequeath them to
~~The good~~ library, ~~darkness somewhere~~, where they shall be lost
~~They shall be lost.~~   ~~But tonight~~ I will take One day, though, I may ~~the~~
~~Out of the~~   ~~I used to hold~~ the manuscript
5   Of Eugene's final composition ~~now and then,~~ out —
And let my eye run down the spidery
Calligraphy of ~~the~~ notes. The small ~~black~~ black things
Would climb the staves slowly or float above
The ~~F~~-line

     The Elegy —   and let my eye rove down
The spidery calligraphy of the notes.
~~The small black notes~~
~~And~~ I watch the ~~small~~ black notes climb up the staves /~~climbing~~
To float above the line like tiny storm-clouds, only
10   Only to dissolve and scatter, ~~like birds~~ /~~birdlike~~ windblown;
And I ~~will~~ hear the sounds behind ~~the notes~~ marks
~~But faintly, as though~~
     like ... , wheeling

At my own pace I can pick out the notes
~~for~~   Of the piano part, but ~~the~~ where is there a cellist
This side of the causeway? And who plays Bestor now?
15   This time of day I listen to the surf
Myself. I sit and listen from my terrace.
~~Perhaps~~
(Does anyone know Bonnard's "La Grande Terrasse"?)
The sun eases its way down, scattering hues,
Beyond the potted palm and potted orange.
~~And I hear~~ The music better here than at the keyboard.

2. The first draft of the poem that developed into the title piece of The Sunset Maker *began as a straightforward translation of prose fiction into blank verse. Justice then spent successive days revising and expanding the typescript by hand, in red ink on 9 February and green ink on 10 February. "I rarely know beforehand where a poem is going to end," he once remarked, and his manuscript notes clearly illustrate this fluidity. Though the lines quickly move away from the original story's language, there is only a hint of the poem's eventual conclusion. This occurs in the scribbled line in the right-hand margin that reads, "Music and painting—the end/heart of life." After many drafts, this concept will become the assertion of art's primacy that brings* "The Sunset Maker" *to its triumphant close.*

3. "The Sunset Maker" *appeared as "Elegy for Cello and Piano" in the* Iowa Review *in 1986. This first published version is nearly identical to the poem's final book form. Though Justice's marginal notes are extensive, he makes only a few changes. Most of these are minor, except for two revisions that emerge from the manuscript jottings at the bottom right-hand side of the leaf. First, Justice transposes the music, raising the pitch of the notes so that they now visually correspond to his description of their "Flying above the staff like flags of mourning." Then, he twice tests the poem's new title.*

Elegy for Cello and Piano · *Donald Justice*

The Bestor papers have come down to me.
I would imagine, though, they're destined for
The quiet archival twilight of some library.
Meanwhile, I have been sorting through the scores.
The ones I linger over is the last,
The 'Elegy.' I seem to see the notes
Flying above the staff like flags of mourning;
And I can hear the sounds the notes intended.
(Some duo of the mind produces them,
Without error, ghost-music materializing;
Faintly, of course, like whispers overheard.)
And then? I might work up the piano part,
Not that it matters. Where is there a cellist
This side of the causeway? And who plays Bestor now?

This time of day I listen to the surf
Myself; I listen to it from my terrace.
The sun eases its way down through the palms,
Scattering colors—a bit of orange, some blues.
Do you know that painting of Bonnard's, *The Terrace*?
It shows a water pitcher blossom-ready
And a woman who bends down to the doomed blossoms—
One of the fates, in orange—and then the sea
With its own streaks of orange, harmonious.
It used to hang in the Phillips near the Steinway.
Can anyone call back how the web of sound
The piano and the cello wove together
In the same Phillips not too long ago?
The three plucked final chords—someone might still
Recall, if not the chords, then the effect
They made—as if the air were troubled somehow.
As if . . . but everything there is is that.
The cello had one phrase, an early phrase,
That does stay with me. (It may be mixed by now
With Bonnard's colors.) A brief rush upward, then

A brief subsiding. Can it be abstract?—
As Stravinsky said it must be to be music.
But what if a phrase *could* represent a thought—
Or feeling, should I say?—without existence
Apart from the score where someone catches it:

Inhale, exhale: a drawn-out gasp or sigh.
Falling asleep, I hear it. It is just there.
I don't say what it means. And I agree
It's sentimental to suppose my friend
Survives in just this fragment, this tone-row
A hundred people halfway heard one Sunday
And one of them no more than half remembers.
The hard early years of study, those still,
Sequestered mornings in the studio,
The perfect ear, the technique, the great gift
All have come down to this one ghostly phrase.
And soon nobody will recall the sound
These six notes made once or that there were six.

Hear the gulls. That's our local music.
I like it myself; and, as you can see,
Our sunset maker studied with Bonnard.

Philip Levine

"I began writing poetry," Philip Levine explains, "to effect some kind of moral change." Convinced that "we live at the pleasure of people with enormous power and very little compassion," Levine urges deeper human sympathy by voicing the anger, pain, and joys of America's exploited classes. His latest collection, *A Walk with Tom Jefferson* (1988), typifies his commitment to the dispossessed lives of the nation's urban laborers. The book explores, he says, "the way we work and don't work in a society that has abandoned so many of its citizens, and how we endure, since that is the only choice we have." Its title poem catches the taut play of Levine's imagination between the extremes of private courage and public despair. In colloquial language, it tells the story of Tom Jefferson, a black man and second-generation victim of "the $5 day that lured/his father from the cotton fields" of the South to Michigan's auto factories. He now inhabits a Detroit slum, whose devastation represents for Levine the irremediable injustice of America's socioeconomic system. Though powerless to improve his condition, Tom Jefferson bravely remains "a believer," reflecting the poet's own romantic faith in the boundless strength of the human spirit.

Himself a son of Detroit's grim industrial landscapes, Levine was born in the city in 1928 of Russian-Jewish parents and grew up attending its schools, eventually taking both bachelor's and master's degrees at Wayne State University. His obsession with the politics of daily life began as a young boy on Detroit's streets. The anti-Semitism he suffered there heightened his awareness of fascism and made childhood heroes of the Republican soldiers in Spain's Civil War. Then at thirteen, he listened with close attention to the radical ideas of neighborhood socialists and anarchists. Their call for "the end of ownership" evolved into his own personal creed a year later, when he took the night shift on Cadillac's assembly line. Faced with "the extraordinary physical agony" of manual labor, Levine understood firsthand the exploitive power of capitalism.

Through adolescence and into his early twenties, Levine continued at "an incredible variety of dumb jobs," which convinced him "that there is very little justice in the world, and that most of what young people are told…about the nature of this country, this America, is nonsense." At twenty-three, certain that the Korean War was being fought "just to advance the American market," he refused the draft. By twenty-six Levine knew that he wanted to devote his life to poetry. During the previous year he had travelled to Iowa City and informally attended the classes of Robert Lowell and John Berryman in the Iowa Writers Workshop. Now he decided to leave Detroit and dedicate himself "to poverty and poetry." In 1957 Levine earned his M.F.A. at Iowa and shortly afterwards left for Stanford to study with Yvor Winters. As his Stanford fellowship ended, Levine accepted a faculty post with California State University at Fresno and has taught creative writing there, on and off, ever since.

In 1963 at age thirty-five, Levine published his first book of poetry, *On the Edge*. Since then he has written steadily, producing twelve major collections over the last twenty-five years. Though wonderfully diverse in occasions and techniques, this varied body of work is unified by Levine's conviction that "being a poet is, in a sense, a political act." At issue is neither party doctrine nor social philosophy—both of which Levine distrusts. Rather his art seeks a humane understanding beyond ideology's easy answers. "We now exist," he explains, "in the kind of world Orwell was predicting, and the simple insistence upon accurate language has become a political act." His is a politics of compassion, relying on the clarity of fact to evoke a sympathy that breaks down the cultural barriers erected by America's economy. Supporting this agenda is Levine's highly accessible style, which avoids the obscurities of much contemporary verse and appeals democratically to a broader reading public. "In my ideal poem, no words are noticed. You look through them," he says, "into a vision of…the people, the place."

Not This Pig (1968) and *Red Dust* (1971) followed *On the Edge*. These early books bitterly trace the "the gradual decay of dignity" among the abused victims of society. Many of the poems are, indeed, "on the edge," alternately raging against the marketplace's wholesale bartering of life and despairing that there is nothing "to choose/but failure." *Not This Pig* and *Red Dust*, along with *Pili's Wall* (1971), also reflect Levine's residence in Spain during the mid-1960s. They at once incorporate incidents from those years and introduce a charged, surreal imagery he learned from Spanish poets. Levine's early work culminates in the riveting energy of *They Feed They Lion* (1972). The book's widely anthologized title poem splices syntactic ambiguity with black gospel rhythms to express the raw, exhilarating anger that provoked Detroit's 1967 racial insurrection.

Levine addresses a different kind of devastation in his next collection, *1933* (1974), which takes its title from the year of his father's death. The book responds elegiacally not only to his particular loss but also to the general "impermanence of growing up in a modern city." Recalling a visit to Detroit, Levine says: "The past disappears in a moment. I could not find the house in which I was born, the schools I went to as a child are torn down, the people I knew dispersed." The instability of urban America horrifies Levine, and its ravages he considers a primary challenge to his art. "One of the earliest motives in my writing," he explains, "was an effort to slow down this voracious eating of time of everything I cared for."

The collections that immediately followed *1933* consolidated Levine's vision and secured his reputation. *The Names of the Lost* won the Lenore Marshall Award for the best book of poetry published by an American in 1976. *Ashes* (1979) and *7 Years from Somewhere* (1979) both received the National Book Critics Circle Award, while *Ashes* was also voted the American Book Award in 1980. At this point, Levine was known mainly as a prophet of a desolate world with scant solace. Typical is Hayden Carruth's characterization of the "*constancy* " of Levine's sensibility—"the bitterness steady from book to book, the grief for blight and poverty and violence."

Levine had, however, always wanted "to be a poet of joy as well as suffering," but not until *One for the Rose* (1981) and *Sweet Will* (1985) did optimism break decisively through the burden of moral indignation. Such transcendent moments of faith in "a world/that runs on and on at its own sweet will," are not, however, easily accomplished. Some of these poems open "with the smell/of defeat" and move slowly into despair before suddenly transfiguring their anger into triumphant defiance. Others reach their celebratory note by absorbing the city's blight into nature's beauty. Particularly moving is "Rain Downriver," where Levine begins with a depressing industrial slum and concludes in radiant tranquility: "From a sky I can/no longer see, the fall of evening/glistens around my shoulders that/also glisten, and the world is mine." This lovely end to alienation opens a new dimension in the politics of human charity that Levine's art has pursued for more than three decades. For it suggests that in its completest form, compassion enables us to repossess spiritually a world that is otherwise hopelessly locked in the grip of economic power.

My first night in California I spent in a motel in Squaw Valley; it was 1957, and the place was being "developed" for the coming winter Olympics, but in August it was all but deserted. I was alone, having left my wife and two sons in Boulder with my mother-in-law while I came ahead to find a place to live. I'd come down with some sort of flu the day before and had stopped early just west of Salt Lake City and slept for twelve hours during which the fever broke. Taking a small AM/FM radio into my Squaw Valley Motel room I felt light-headed and slightly high on nothing. On an FM station from Berkeley I found the most amazing radio program I'd ever heard; it consisted of one man with an extraordinarily affected and ponderous academic voice reminiscing on the famous he'd known. His articularity and the range of his associations bedazzled me: Gertrude Stein, Jung, Robinson Jeffers, Isaac Bashevis Singer, Luis Companys, Tu Fu. It turned out to be Kenneth Rexroth, a true poet on the radio! What a rich world I'd stumbled into. I was so excited I had trouble sleeping that night and rose and dressed while it was still dark. By noon I'd crossed the Bay Bridge into San Francisco and headed down the peninsula for Los Altos and the home of Yvor Winters, who had generously offered to put me up until I found a place to live.

That spring I'd received a short terse letter from Winters informing me that he'd chosen me to receive a Stanford Writing Fellowship. This was a great relief for my wife and me; our second son had come down with a childhood form of asthma, and we were advised to seek a more gentle climate than the Midwest offered. For two years I'd been teaching Technical Writing in the Engineering College of the University of Iowa, and it left me with very little time for my own writing; it was the first job I'd had that left my hands clean, and I'd begun to wonder if I could both live on my wits and write poetry, for I'd written more while doing slave work in Detroit.

Winters' home on Portola Road was surrounded by a high redwood fence, and a sign on the gate warned that there were dangerous dogs within. I advanced gingerly. The door was answered by a tall, spare woman whom I'd interrupted at household chores; I took her to be the maid. Her hair was drawn back and largely hidden under a flowered scarf; when I told her why I'd come she gave me a wonderful open and welcoming smile. I recalled a little magical poem by Winters' wife, the poet and novelist Janet Lewis, which depicted the slow movements of just such a woman, and I wondered if, like "some Elsie" of W.C. Williams' famous poem, she were the same maid grown to adulthood.

GIRL HELP Janet Lewis

Mild and slow and young,
She moves about the room,
And stirs the summer dust
With her wide broom.

In the warm, lofted air,
Soft lips together pressed,
Soft wispy hair
She stops to rest.

And stops to breathe,
Amid the summer hum,
The great white lilac bloom
Scented with days to come.

Seated, waiting for the arrival of my mentor-to-be, I noticed a photo of Winters on a bookshelf behind the television set. (Did Yvor Winters actually watch television?) The woman in the photo alongside Winters was this very housekeeper, who I suddenly realized must be Janet Lewis.

During my year at Stanford I learned that Winters did indeed watch tv, for he was a fanatical fan of prize fighting. I too was a boxing fan, and this brought us together at least once a week at his home to watch the Friday Night Fights, on which we usually bet when there was a difference of opinion. In my incredibly short career as a boxer I'd learned considerably more about fighting than Winters knew, and I never lost a bet to him, although the largest I ever won was a quarter. Like many Californians of that era, Winters was a hater of some actual or imagined Eastern fight establishment which had managed to keep deserving Western fighters permanently from glory. He especially hated Floyd Patterson, who was not part of any establishment but who had refused to give the new California hope, Eddie Machen, a shot at the heavyweight title. (Machen finally got his big chance against Ingemar Johansson and was knocked out in the first round.) In other words, Winters felt about prize fighting exactly as he did about poetry—it was rigged by some invisible, all-powerful Eastern force, and he and his "discoveries" would have to wait on the outside pending some miracle.

In Iowa we had been living rather poorly but surviving on my job, which paid $3600 the second year—I'd gotten a $100 raise after the first year—but my rent in Iowa City had been $60 a month. Palo Alto was something else. At the Stanford housing office I discovered the listings were totally out of my reach—I remember one house that came complete with pool and gardener, was suitable for four (which we were), and went for $700 a month, which would have devoured my entire fellowship. In East Palo Alto near the Southern Pacific tracks I found a second-floor apartment that went for $125 and took it with a sense of relief. On my first day on campus as a graduate fellow an event occurred that set the tone for the entire year. I had come expressly to the office of scholarships to claim my first quarter's check and I'd dressed in what I'd thought would be the costume of a Stanford student of some years (29) and considerable dignity. To myself I was invisible among the lively throng of students. To my horror a man

wearing the uniform of a Railway Express Driver sidled up and addressed me as an intimate. "Let me tell you, friend," he said, "don't ever deliver trunks to this place. They make you haul them up three flights and tip you nothing." What was it about me that revealed who I was, a former driver for Railway Express? I drove home in shock to ask my wife that question, but she assured me it was merely a coincidence, and I looked like what I was, a poet.

Before the end of the fall quarter I was broke and took a job at the Post Office, where after a few days of sorting mail under surveillance (I could see nothing to steal), I was assigned to delivering mail to a large new, very stylish housing tract. For this I was equipped with a heavy and awkward bicycle with a tiny front wheel over which rose a wooden box in which the mail was stashed. The regular who broke me in advised me never to complete the route on time because I was new and should take at least two hours more than he, which left half the afternoon for reading. He also warned me against the dogs which roamed the deserted afternoon streets at their pleasure, and one dog in particular, an attack dog owned by a former military officer who refused to leash or restrain him. When he was on the loose I was to avoid the entire block and return the mail undelivered. Winters urged on me a water gun filled with Clorox; it had worked for him when he'd bicycled to Stanford in years past. Amazingly it worked far better than the stones I'd been using.

By mid-January the holiday crush had passed, and I was out of work, but the second quarter's check rescued us. Out of the blue my brother called asking if I'd like to work for him purchasing bearings the government was offering for sale. He sent me long lists of what he was interested in, and I viewed the bearings at various military depots such as the Oakland Navy Yard and the army warehouses at Benicia, phoned him about their condition, and then submitted his bids. If he was awarded it was my job to see that the material was properly packed and shipped to Detroit. I'm not sure why I hated the job so much. Perhaps it was from a sense that at any moment we could be cheated, that inferior material would be substituted the first time I looked away. I had the idea that people were waiting to be bribed, but was unsure and had no idea how one would go about offering a bribe. My brother, an identical twin, moved among such men with an assurance and bravado that totally escaped me, and although he promised me a large

percentage of the take, in the end I received my expenses and a few dollars an hour.

That spring Fresno State offered me an instructorship teaching creative writing, composition and literature; they also offered me enough money to live on. Stanford countered with an offer of a teaching fellowship to work on my doctorate, a degree I felt no great need of. I was too old to be a student, and I was tired of being treated as one. I had belonged to the CIO, the AF of L, the Teamsters, the Brotherhood of Railway Workers, and I was finding it impossible to pretend respect for those for whom I felt none. I never had that problem with Winters. I respected him enormously; he was the most deeply serious man I had ever met, and he was profoundly egalitarian in the way that only men and women of enormous self-confidence can afford to be. He never treated me as anything but an equal, although he spent hours trying to educate me on such subjects as the wines of California, the proper methods for making olives palatable, the varieties of fruit-bearing trees that graced his gardens, the development of poetry in English, the beauties of Mexican culture, and the power and purity of the poetry of Baudelaire, Valéry, and Tristan Corbière. In these private sessions he was a generous and inspired teacher. He was in fact a tender and gentle man under his clumsy and gruff exterior which tended to ward off those displays of affection that embarrassed him. I hope he grasped my enduring thankfulness—never openly expressed—to both him and Janet for all they gave and for welcoming me to the West.

Philip Levine

Selected Works by Philip Levine

Poetry

On the Edge. Iowa City: Stone Wall Press, 1963.
Not This Pig. Middletown: Wesleyan University Press, 1968.
Pili's Wall. Santa Barbara: Unicorn Press, 1971.
Red Dust. Santa Cruz: Kayak, 1971.
They Feed They Lion. New York: Atheneum, 1972.
1933. New York: Atheneum, 1974.
The Names of the Lost. New York: Atheneum, 1976.
7 Years from Somewhere. New York: Atheneum, 1979.
Ashes: Poems New and Old. New York: Atheneum, 1979.
One for the Rose. New York: Atheneum, 1981.
Selected Poems. New York: Atheneum, 1984.
Sweet Will. New York: Atheneum, 1985.
A Walk with Tom Jefferson. New York: Knopf, 1988.

Other

Don't Ask (interviews). Ann Arbor: University of Michigan Press, 1981.

Editor, *The Essential Keats.* New York: Ecco Press, 1987.

1.

Philip Levine was twenty-eight years old in the summer of 1957 when he arrived at Stanford to study with Yvor Winters. In interviews Levine has discussed their aesthetic conflicts, remarking how Winters "loathed my poetry" and explaining his own objections to Winters's neoclassical "'right reason.'" But Levine also recognized in Winters a "terribly clumsy" man who "wanted to be kind, and…didn't quite know how." Despite their differences, the two became friends. Nearly thirty years elapsed, however, before Levine returned imaginatively to his first year in California and commemorated that friendship in "28." The poem first appeared in the New Yorker *in 1986 and then was collected in* A Walk with Tom Jefferson *(1988).*

1. Levine typically works quickly. "I can write the first draft—when I'm hot—in twenty minutes, and two hours later I've gone through six drastic revisions and the poem is finished." This draft of "28" reflects Levine's usual practice, with the poem developing fully in two separate bursts of creative energy. The first stage begins in mid-page, after a series of phrases and images that act like warm-up exercises. Composition then proceeds confidently for another two pages. Only occasional revisions break the flow, before the writing comes to a complete halt in a group of rejected lines on the fourth page. Here Levine's memory seems to have been so dense with detail that he momentarily lost the poem's narrative thrust. To recover his direction, Levine jots in prose several ideas about Winters and outlines the poem's thematic scheme: "Bring them all together, " he tells himself, "First trip West, the crash—death, the soul."

of ground cinders, pebbles, rough grass.
                                        at twice my age
Arthur, too, was faithless, or so he insisted
through the long sober evenings in Los Altos, once
crowded with the cries of coyotes. His face
darkened and his fists shook when he spoke
of Nothing, what he would become in that waiting blaze
of final cold, a whiteness like no other.
At 56, more scared of me than I of him,
his right forefinger raised to keep the beat,
he gravelled out his two great gifts of truth:
"I'd rather die than reread the last novels
of Henry James," and, "Philip, we must never lie
or we shall lose our souls." All one winter afternoon
he chanted in Breton French the coarse poems of Tristan Corbiere,
his voice reaching into unforseen sweetness, both hands
rising to the ceiling, the tears held back so long
still held back, for he was dying and he was happy.

By April I had crossed the Pacheco Pass and found
roosting in the dark branches of the Joshua tree
the fabled magpie--"had a long tongue and a long tail,
he could both talk and do"--. This is a holy land,
I thought. At a Sonoco station the attendant,
wirey and dour, said in perfect Okie, "be careful, son,
a whole family was wiped out right here
just yesterday." At Berenda the fields were flooded
for miles in every direction. Arthur's blank sky
scared down at an unruffled inland sea and threatened
to let go. On the way home I cut lilacs
from the divider strip of El Camino Real.
My wife was pregnant. All night we hugged
each other in our narrow bed as the rain
came on in sheets. A family of five, and all
of us were out of work. The dawn was silent.
The black roses, battered, unclenched, the burned petals
floated on the pond beside the play house.
Beneath the surface the tiny stunned pike circled
no prey we could see. That was not another life.
I was 29 now and faithless, not the father of the man
I am but the same man who all this day
sat in a still house watching the low clouds massing
in the west, the new winds coming on.
By late afternoon the kids are home from school,
clambering on my front porch, though day
after day I beg them not to. When I go
to the window they race off in mock horror,
daring me to follow. The huge crows that wake
me every morning settle back on the rainspout
next door to caw to the season. The 8 year old
with a cap of blond hair falling to her shoulders
darts between parked cars and for no reason
suddenly cartwheeels into the early dusk.

2.

3.

2. The draft's second stage carries "28" to its conclusion. The speed of Levine's creative practice is evident in his technique of immediate revision. The brackets on these pages enclose passages that dissatisfied him at the time of composition. Rather than defer them to a later draft, he rewrites on the spot, often achieving lines that continue virtually unchanged into the poem's final version. These junctures also illuminate another aspect of Levine's method. "Usually for me," he explains, "the act of writing is the act of discovery." And, indeed, Levine seldom deletes the bracketed lines; rather, he usually discovers additional material that improves the original lines by enriching their meaning. This process is evident at the draft's close, where Levine first brackets and expands the image of the eight-year-old girl, then introduces the new figure of the crows, inserting it into the text above the revised lines.

3. The typescript essentially transcribes Levine's manuscript draft with only minor differences. The longhand revisions that follow are in black, brown, and red ink, indicating the separate occasions on which Levine reviewed his typescript. These changes are also minor, except for another new passage at the poem's conclusion. At this point "28" is almost identical to its printed form, though Levine still continued to revise, making small shifts in diction. Interestingly, these can sometimes carry important thematic implications—such as Levine's altering a single word in his farewell line to Winters. The typescript's phrase, "for he was dying and he was happy," reads in the final printed version, "for he was dying and he was ready," thus subtly but significantly refocusing the poem's image of Winters.

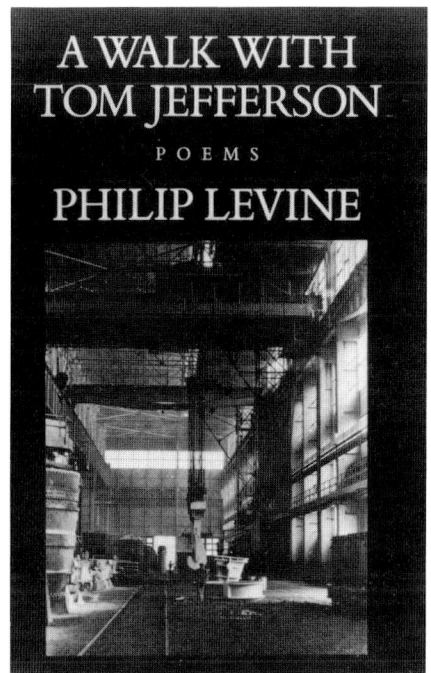

A WALK WITH TOM JEFFERSON

POEMS

PHILIP LEVINE

Thomas McGuane

Thomas McGuane writes with wit and compassion about psychic survival in contemporary America. Many of the male protagonists of his novels are manic figures, who scandalize public decorum and inflict their anger on those dearest to them. The values that impel these crazed, unconventional lives are, however, familiar elements of our national tradition—masculine honor and self-reliance, romantic love and marriage, the security and support of family, the sportsman's respect for nature. But the ground for such old-fashioned values has, in McGuane's view, long since been eroded by the country's vulgar wealth, political cynicism, and complacent self-absorption. "The America you see in public," he comments, "is the monster who crawls to the door in the middle of the night and must be driven back to the end of the driveway." To keep that beast at bay is the principal challenge of McGuane's starkly unsentimental art. How difficult and prone to failure is that task, he knows all too well, having endured its trials as both a writer and a man.

McGuane was born in 1939 in Wyandotte, Michigan, the son of a poor Boston Irishman who went through Harvard on scholarship before migrating to the Midwest to start a successful auto-parts company. A laconic, hard-driving workaholic, McGuane's father neglected the family as his obsession with business increased. This was, McGuane says, an "inconsolable" loss that he lamented "for a big part of my life." In contrast, his mother's family, also Irish Catholic immigrants, were a warm, garrulous, back-slapping clan. "Actually, I derive myself matrilineally," McGuane says. But this happier heritage could not prevent the shattering effects of his father's distance. "My sister died of a drug overdose in her middle twenties; my brother has been a custodial case since he was thirty; as soon as my mother was given the full reins of her own life, after my dad died, she drank herself to death in thirty-six months." This tragic unravelling was McGuane's firsthand education in the vicious underside of the American dream, and elements of it regularly occur in his fiction.

While still at prep school, McGuane decided to be a writer and by sixteen was already working at it daily. Since writing was not a practical career, he tried several pre-professional courses at Michigan State before finally settling on a degree in English. An M.F.A. in playwriting from the Yale School of Drama preceded his coming to Stanford in 1966 as a Stegner Fellow in fiction. Throughout these years McGuane was so desperate to be a good writer and so fearful of failure that he disciplined himself fanatically, often working "six or seven days a week, nine or ten hours a day." Before arriving at Stanford he had already drafted several books, though "all that stuff," he explains, "was going in the closet." But during the next six years, McGuane's "insane dedication" paid off, and he published three novels, all to high critical praise.

The first two, *The Sporting Club* (1968) and *The Bushwhacked Piano* (1971), are comic extravaganzas that brilliantly satirize contemporary America. McGuane describes *The Sporting Club* as an "anarchist tract" that uses a snobbish hunting and fishing lodge as a political paradigm of the Republic. Vernor Stanton, the novel's chaotically energetic hero, typifies McGuane's protagonists. Though as privileged as the club's other members, Stanton despises them and plots a series of assaults on their staid gentility, climaxed by arranging a violent invasion of lower-class toughs. His revolution devastates the club, but it also inflicts severe psychological damage on him. Nicholas Payne, *The Bushwhacked Piano* 's young renegade from surburbia, also pays dearly for his rebellion, in this case against middle-class banality. On a lunatic odyssey from Detroit to Montana to Key West in search of love and personal meaning, he encounters a gallery of American grotesques, who demonstrate with brutal humor the mindless venality of rich and poor alike. At the end of his journey through our "declining snivelization," Payne's only possessions are the freedom born of disillusionment and a stubborn will to enjoy it.

In his third novel, *Ninety-Two in the Shade* (1973), McGuane sharply increases the cost of nonconformity. Thomas Skelton, whose spiritual desolation mirrors America's cultural bankruptcy, retreats to his home in Key West after another empty drug high. There he discovers in the craft of the professional fishing guide an escape from his personal nightmare. But in the strained economy of Skelton's emotional life, any compromise of his newly found sense of honor is impossible, an inflexibility that leads to his murder. With this tragic tale McGuane moved his art away from satiric flash. *Ninety-Two in the Shade*, he comments, "was the first of the books in which I felt I brought my personal sense of epochal crisis to my interest in literature." Critics agreed, nominating it for the National Book Award.

But before McGuane started another novel, this epochal crisis erupted in his own life. A near-fatal accident, when his Porsche ricocheted off a truck at 140 miles an hour, unstrung him. To continue "being a control freak...always in the damn library" now became unthinkable, and McGuane dropped his routine of daily writing for a reckless spree in Hollywood that earned him the nickname "Captain Beserko." Two divorces, a lot of drinking, some drugs, and then, within thirty-six months, the deaths of his mother, father, and sister left McGuane burnt out. This was "big trouble," he says, but eventually it proved to be "good trouble." For, after McGuane's life was stabilized by his marriage to Laurie Buffett in 1977 and their return to his Montana ranch, the trauma of those years broadened and matured McGuane's sensibility. The first sign of this advance was *Panama* (1978), the disturbing cautionary tale of Chet Pomeroy, a wildly successful but self-destructive performance artist whose career willfully incorporates the national hysteria of the 1970s. "I was making a tremendous living," Pomeroy says, "demonstrating, with the aplomb of a Fuller Brush salesman, all the nightmares, all the loathsome, toppling states of mind, all the evil things that go on behind closed eyes."

Four years later, McGuane followed *Panama* 's vision of monstrous emptiness and excess with *Nobody's Angel* (1982), a very different novel, which recovers the sense of loss that sometimes breaks through the comic surfaces of his earlier work. McGuane's themes are again the failure of love and family, but he now draws on older characters whose lives are deeply enmeshed in social obligations. The result is a new emotional resonance. New as well is *Nobody's Angel* 's geographical location in Deadrock, Montana, a fictional town modelled on Livingston, which is near McGuane's 3,000-acre Raw Deal Ranch. Deadrock figures in many of the short stories in his most recent book, *To Skin a Cat* (1986), and is also the setting of his latest novel, *Something to Be Desired* (1984), which satirically explores "a piece of crazy venture capitalism" as an emblem of the "American approach to desperation." But although Montana is now home to McGuane both literally and artistically, it is no nostalgic refuge of bygone virtues. Despite the rugged splendor of its landscape, Deadrock has been overrun by the New West's crass commercialism. Like the gentrified Centennial Club of McGuane's first novel, it serves as a symbolic scene for his ongoing test of sanity's chances for survival in contemporary America.

I note a couple of decades have passed. The gentle slope looks well to become a precipice. I have not been back to Stanford since my year there, 1966, and my memory of that time is undisturbed. If I returned, I would expect to find a demonstration against the war in Vietnam in progress; I would expect a production of Big Brother and the Holding Company to be available to me; and I would expect to feel that constant stomach-centered fear that I associate with an apprenticeship in letters.

My contemporaries were talented. California was startling. I had friends with meditation rooms. My first week, a former writing fellow had me over to drink orange juice and listen to Ravi Shankar and Ali Akbar Khan. Another, on leave from the State Department, asked me from a great altitude who my agent was. In trying to find housing where my bird dog would also be welcome, I was informed by a realtor that "dogs make feces." I bought a motorcycle. As I listened to others of the young writers read, I came to feel well down on the food chain, and the discomfort inside grew.

I was interested in the history of the picaresque novels of Lazarillo de Tormes, Defoe, Fielding, Gogol, Cervantes, and Sterne, and loved their rough, strung-together architecture and forceful prose. I made room for Dean Swift because of his wit and meanness; it would have been nice if I'd gotten his prose as well. These were not universal concerns in the writing seminars of the `60s. It was more acceptable to speak to one's race or politics. In a writing seminar with a slightly western twang, I wasn't even the son of a rancher or cowboy. My middle-class midwestern origins seemed slim pickings. Furthermore, there was little interest in those days among young writers in literature. Those of us who had come out of the land-grant schools of the middle of the nation hadn't got the news yet. We were still in the Fifties, really. To us, literature was religion, the more self-enclosed, and the more hieratic its practitioners, the better. No meditation rooms in East Lansing, and no Ravi Shankar on the radio coming home from the drag races at Flat Rock. The sophisticated former writing student who still hung around the campus told me that Jorge Luis Borges typified the excesses of the provinces. I quietly hoped my own origins qualified me similarly. One goes further and further to find a pulse.

Looking back, that pulse lay in fear and unspecific hunger, things which thrive anywhere. The palms, the opulence, the purposeful faculty of Stanford, only threw fat on the fire. The young writer is a sojourner who can turn the most comfortable landscape into desert.

Thomas McGuane

Selected Works by Thomas McGuane

Fiction

The Sporting Club. New York: Simon and Schuster, 1968.
The Bushwhacked Piano. New York: Simon and Schuster, 1971.
Ninety-Two in the Shade. New York: Farrar Straus Giroux, 1973.
Panama. New York: Farrar Straus Giroux, 1978.
Nobody's Angel. New York: Random House, 1982.
Something to Be Desired. New York: Random House, 1984.
To Skin a Cat. New York: Dutton, 1986.

Other

An Outside Chance: Essays on Sport. New York: Farrar Straus Giroux, 1980.

Individual Interviews

Alive and Writing: Interviews with American Authors of the 1980s, with Larry McCaffery and Sinda Gregory. Urbana: University of Illinois Press, 1987.
"A Conversation with Tom McGuane," with Liz Lear. *Shenandoah,* 36.2 1986.
"An Interview with Tom McGuane," with Kay Bonetti. *Missouri Review,* 9.1 1985-86.
"Thomas McGuane: An Interview," with Albert Howard Carter, III. *Fiction International,* 4/5 1975.

When Thomas McGuane came to Stanford, he says, "I had with me a novel called The Fire Season, *whose only merit lay in having been drafted at all. R.W.B. Lewis offered to discuss it, then broke his appointment. William Styron offered to send it to his publisher, as long as he didn't have to read it.... A few years later, I found what I needed in the manuscript of* The Fire Season, *a name, a couple of phrases. What was saveable from a few hundred hand written pages went handily on a matchbook cover."*

1. The Fire Season *was originally written in three notebooks, beginning in the summer of 1964 while McGuane was traveling in Ireland. There were, he explains, "almost no corrected lines in the manuscript because I was less interested in good prose than in getting to the end." The typescript confirms this, virtually duplicating the manuscript word for word. But there were exceptions, such as the passage where Nicholas Payne,* The Fire Season's *main character, discovers in a gulch a piano splintered by bullets. This scene engaged McGuane deeply enough to prompt major revisions between manuscript and typescript. Among these changes was McGuane's new description of the piano as "bushwhacked." This image, along with Payne's name, would be all that he salvaged from the novel.*

1.

2. With The Fire Season *behind him, McGuane opened a new notebook, listing on its first pages the titles of forty-five possible stories, starting with* The Piano in the Gulch. *On subsequent pages he then sketched possible plot elements and themes for his next novel. On the right-hand page displayed here, McGuane diagrams an intersection between "The Comic Strain" and "The Magic Strain" in a love story involving a man named Quinn and his girlfriend, Ann. As the notebook proceeds, McGuane changes the male character's name to Nicholas Payne and reworks the initial outline into* The Bushwhacked Piano, *which does, in fact, open by recalling* The Fire Season *'s bullet-riddled piano.*

(The COMIC STRAIN) (The MAGIC STRAIN)

The love conceit
The counter-conceit of Quinn & his band
The smaller conceits involving the mother, father
   and brother of the girl.
Quinn's own family
Quinn's competitor: the pregnancy denouement
Quinn's occupation: how, specifically, is
   it to be dealt with.
A. Just released from the Navy, he
   hasn't started the next thing yet.

The tragic denouement would be the loss
of the girl. A comic denouement would
be (avoiding the farcical happily-ever-after)
his disillusionment with her.

Back to the old idea of wrecking his
aspirations through his behavior.

Walk-In The-Water
Opening: Travelling downriver. homecoming.

The long sentence.

2.

Larry McMurtry

Larry McMurtry's fiction focuses on his home state of Texas, where his family has lived for four generations. It was in 1877 that his grandfather, William Jefferson McMurtry, first rode into the Panhandle with his wife Louisa Francis and bought a half-section of land in Archer County at three dollars an acre. At the time, the U.S. cavalry was still subduing the Comanches, and cattle drives cut through Archer County from Fort Belknap to Buffalo Springs. But when McMurtry was born in 1936, those rugged days had already receded into the past. They lived on for McMurtry only in the stories and the dreams of his uncles, who "were cowboys first and last."

As a boy on the family ranch near Wichita Falls, McMurtry was not particularly interested in writing. "I grew up," he says, "in a bookless town, in a bookless part of the state—when I stepped into a university library, at age eighteen, the whole of the world's literature lay before me unread, a country as vast, as promising, and so far as I knew, as trackless as the West must have seemed to the first white men who looked upon it." In fact McMurtry did not think much about writing until he was twenty-one. Then, during his junior and senior years at North Texas State College, he produced more than fifty short stories, although eventually he burned them all. McMurtry remained dissatisfied with his work until he turned his imaginative eye toward home and wrote two stories set on a ranch like the one of his childhood. While taking his master's degree in English at Rice University, he combined the two stories and expanded them into a draft of his first novel, *Horseman, Pass By* (1961). That same year he completed a draft of his second novel, *Leaving Cheyenne* (1963), and he brought both of the manuscripts with him when he came to Stanford in 1960 as a Stegner Fellow.

These two early novels embody McMurtry's vision of contemporary life on the West Texas plains. He had seen "the ideals of the [cowboy] faith degenerate, the rituals fall from use, the principal myth become corrupt," and his fiction dramatically recreates this decline of heroic values into mean-spirited opportunism. In *Horseman, Pass By*, the opposing sides are represented by Homer Bannon and his stepson, Hud. Bannon is an old-style cattle rancher, slow to act and resigned to nature's trials; Hud is a Cadillac cowboy, impatient for wealth and ready for violence. In the two men's struggle to gain influence over the family and control the ranch, McMurtry captures the passing of Texas's traditional values.

Horseman, Pass By and *Leaving Cheyenne* are both set in the outskirts of the fictional town of Thalia. In his third book, *The Last Picture Show* (1966), McMurtry describes this small Texas community in poignant detail. The closing of the local movie theater signals the town's steady decay and increasing isolation. Helplessly trapped in Thalia, the characters endure lives of frustrated dreams and reckless emotions. The three novels form a triptych, together tracing, McMurtry explains, "the large social action that I observed as I grew up, which was the move off the land toward the cities and the gradual disintegration of the rural way of life, and the small-town way of life, too."

Ironically, as McMurtry's early novels were recording this exodus, he made an identical move. At the beginning of the 1970s, he uprooted himself from Texas and settled in Washington D. C., where he still owns and operates the antiquarian book shop Booked Up. His next three novels, culminating in *Terms of Endearment* (1977), reflect this change in location. Although their focus is still on Texas, they are narrated from an urban perspective. The characters represent a new generation of Texans, who actively participate in the modern world but are emotionally dominated by the culture of the old West. Displaced even in their own sprawling cities, they live, the critic Janis Stout observes, "with no apparent means of orienting themselves and nothing to engage them but endless, unsatisfying motion."

With the completion of this urban trilogy, McMurtry felt he had imaginatively exhausted the subject of contemporary Texas. "The move off the land is now virtually completed," he notes, "and that was the great subject that Texas offered writers of my generation." Beginning in 1978 McMurtry branched out both geographically and thematically, producing three novels set respectively in Hollywood, Washington, and Las Vegas. Each has picaresque characters, best represented by the title figure of *Cadillac Jack* (1982), who drives from one end of the country to the other in search of antiques and oddities. Many critics found these works less vivid than the earlier novels and complained that they were thematically shallow in comparison to McMurtry's more deeply rooted work on Texas.

In 1985 McMurtry returned his fiction to Texas with *Lonesome Dove*. Having already explored the modern disintegration of the cowboy ethos, he now began retracing the origins of Texas's mythic past in a work of epic scale. Set in the 1870s, this Pulitzer Prize-winning novel follows a single cattle drive from the Rio Grande to Montana. It moves with vivid energy from stampedes through gunfights to lynchings, climaxing in a scene described by Robert Adams in the *New York Review of Books* as "a barbaric, stately, Homeric cortege" that is "Quixotic and absurd, as well as a dazzling piece of imaginative writing."

McMurtry maintains this Western focus in his two most recent novels. *Texasville* (1987), a sequel to *The Last Picture Show*, presents Thalia in the 1980s, where the vestiges of oil boom money are everywhere. The characters, many of whom appeared as adolescents in *The Last Picture Show*, are for the most part sad and broken adults. Their brief immersion in wealth has left nothing but gaudy ugliness in its wake, lending force to McMurtry's conviction that "Texas is rich in unredeemed dreams." *Anything for Billy* (1988) reaches back to the historical past of *Lonesome Dove* and continues McMurtry's reinvention of the frontier world of nineteenth-century America. The novel's central figure derives from the legendary gunfighter Billy the Kid, whose story is told through the eyes of a dime-novel writer. Through this narrative strategy McMurtry foregrounds the conflict between fable and fact and probes fiction's role in creating the myths that dominate our perceptions of the past.

Although in Thalia the movies did not always thrive, McMurtry found success in Hollywood from the outset of his career. Shortly after he left Stanford, Paramount Pictures shot the Academy Award-winning film *Hud*, based on *Horseman, Pass By* and starring Paul Newman. Nearly ten years later, McMurtry and Peter Bogdanovich completed the screenplay of *The Last Picture Show*, for which McMurtry shared an Academy Award for best screen adaptation from another medium. Then in 1984, Paramount's film of *Terms of Endearment*, starring Jack Nicholson, Shirley MacLaine and Debra Winger, won four Academy Awards, including Best Picture. And the successful conversion of McMurtry's fiction into film continued in 1989, when CBS aired a television mini-series of *Lonesome Dove* starring Robert Duvall.

The writing seminar at Stanford in 1960-61 was for me very much the right thing at the right time. What I profited the most from was the intense competitiveness among my fellow seminarists. Everyone in the class obviously wanted to become the best writer in the world and seemed, at first, convinced that their ascension was inevitable. Of course, this competitiveness wasn't to *everyone's* taste; a few frail-spirited sorts went into immediate and permanent decline, but most of us raced along at top speed, eager to earn the pole position in the Indy 500 of Literature. It was thrilling....

Larry McMurtry

Selected Works by Larry McMurtry

Fiction

Horseman, Pass By. New York: Harper & Brothers, 1961.
Leaving Cheyenne. New York: Harper & Row, 1963.
The Last Picture Show. New York: Dial Press, 1966.
Moving On. New York: Simon and Schuster, 1970.
All My Friends Are Going to Be Strangers. New York: Simon and Schuster, 1972.
Terms of Endearment. New York: Simon and Schuster, 1975.
Somebody's Darling. New York: Simon and Schuster, 1978.
Cadillac Jack. New York: Simon and Schuster, 1982.
The Desert Rose. New York: Simon and Schuster, 1983.
Lonesome Dove. New York: Simon and Schuster, 1986.
Texasville. New York: Simon and Schuster, 1987.
Anything For Billy. New York: Simon and Schuster, 1988.

Other

In a Narrow Grave: Essays on Texas. Austin: Encino Press, 1968.
Larry McMurtry: Unredeemed Dreams, edited by Dorey Schmidt. Edinburgh, Texas: Pan American University, 1980.
Film Flam. New York: Simon and Schuster, 1987.

Individual Interviews

Talking with Texas Writers, with Patrick Bennett. College Station: Texas A&M University Press, 1980.
"A Texan Who Deflates Legends of the West," with Mervyn Rothstein. *New York Times,* 1 November 1988.

In April 1960, several months before McMurtry began attending the Creative Writing workshops at Stanford, Harper & Brothers paid him $250 for an option to publish Horseman, Pass By. That contract stipulated "an acceptable revision of the manuscript" and opened a long, difficult correspondence between McMurtry and his editor at Harper, John Leggett.

1. The version of Horseman, Pass By that Leggett originally read was well over 400 pages. In his first letter to McMurtry, dated 7 April 1960, Leggett opened with praise, assuring McMurtry that "you are going to write some fine novels about the panhandle and its people," but then he immediately launched into two single-spaced pages of editorial advice. Here Leggett identifies "the weakest part of the book" as the relationship of the central character, Lonnie, with his mother. In later drafts, McMurtry accepted Leggett's criticism and cut all references to the boy's parents, emphasizing instead his ties to his grandfather, Homer Bannon.

Leggett, reacting to this early typescript, also expresses his dissatisfaction with the novel's climax, in which the hired hand, Jesse, runs Bannon down in a Cadillac and then shoots the injured old man, ostensibly out of mercy. Leggett found the scene "bewildering rather than inevitable," and a close reading confirms his judgment. For Jesse's explanation is sufficiently confused to suggest that McMurtry was himself unclear about the character's motivation.

On loan from the University of Houston Libraries

HARPER & BROTHERS

PUBLISHERS SINCE 1817

49 East 33rd Street, New York 16, N.Y.

Mr. Larry McMurtry   - 2 -   April 7, 1960

Halmea over the checker game. The motivation isn't quite clear to me.

The weakest part of the book is Lonnie's relationship with his mother. I don't believe her for a moment. I don't believe a girl who had an expensive schooling or any schooling could write so inarticulate a letter to her son, and she most certainly would not be giving him a running account of his stepfather's progress with a waitress. I don't actually think Lonnie's father and mother would be an important factor in his behavior. They would have been replaced by Homer and, I guess, Halmea by this time. I hope you'll think about making them of less importance in Lonnie's young manhood.

Also, we never know how Lonnie feels about the ranch - how badly he wants it, what he plans for it, how he feels about its loss. Jesse's influence seems to lose touch with Lonnie throughout the central part of the book so that his astonishing behavior - failing to appear at the rodeo and then mercy killing old Homer - is bewildering rather than inevitable to the reader.

What would you think about making full use of the suspense about the herd - introducing the suspicions about the hoof-and-mouth disease, showing each of the characters' reactions to it, Hud's, Homer's, Jesse's, Lonnie's. (By the way, is it really true there is still no serum for it? Nothing to do but kill the herd?) and holding the actual slaughter until near the end of the book. The rodeo, I'm pretty sure, can be worked in as a denoument and final chapter.

I may have gone on at too great length here and done a good job of alienating you, but I thought it better to risk that and work on the assumption that you have an itch to do some drastic revision on HORSEMAN and would welcome some editorial thoughts.

If you think we might see eye-to-eye on the eventual shape of the novel, you'll find us willing to put down a modest

more . . .

CABLE ADDRESS : HARPSAM   ·   TELEPHONE : MURRAY HILL 3-1900

1.

2.

HORSEMAN,
PASS BY
a novel
Larry McMurtry

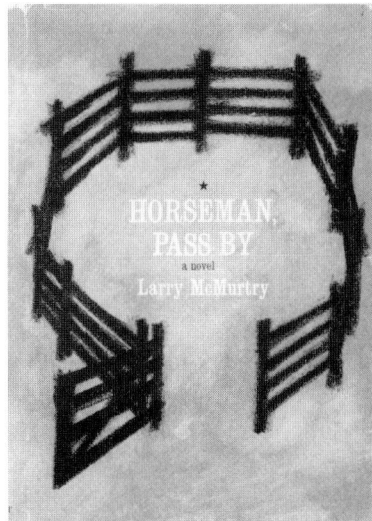

2. In response to Leggett's comments, McMurtry rewrote the climax entirely. By this fifth draft, instead of a ranch hand at the center of the action, Bannon's own stepson Hud is behind the wheel and pulling the trigger. Now, as Hud explains himself, the violent recklessness of his language more effectively registers the anger and frustration that led to the shooting.

Despite McMurtry's major revisions, Leggett remained dissatisfied with the scene. His 23 August 1960 letter insists that Bannon's murder still does not seem "inevitable from what we know of the characters." Leggett also complains about McMurtry's heavy use of profanity and proceeds to list the appearances of vulgar language page by page. "Like garlic", he tells McMurtry, "a little goes a long way."

On loan from the Harry Ransom Humanities Research Center

3.

have seen the light and come down the road and found them, seen his wife with her naked teats and Hud had had to shoot him. I knew he couldn't shoot Hud. I got scared and began to walk faster. I wanted to be out in the light. Then I heard the woman crying something at Hud, and I didn't hear anything else.

4.

When I came into the light, Lily was bent over the turtleback of the big car, crying into her elbow. Hud stood by the fender of the pickup, talking to himself. The bottle of whiskey was sitting on the fender, and the rifle leaned against the pickup door. I saw the ejected shell laying in the dirt road, the brass shining in the light. Hud was talking, to himself, or to Lily, I never did know. Then he drank, his head jerking quickly back.

My granddad lay in the bar ditch. He lay still. An old Levi jacket, the one we kept behind the pickup seat, it had been thrown over his face, so I couldn't see what he looked like, or see his head at all. Lily's dress, the fancy one all white and gold, was stretched over Granddad too; it covered up his side. Just his two bare legs stuck out from under the dress, one straight, and one bent crooked, and scarred up besides from that rope tear years and years before. I knew it was Granddad there dead, but I kept thinking it wasn't. I saw some blood puddled in the gravel by the Levi jacket, and I choked and gagged. But I didn't get sick. I went over and squatted down by Granddad, by the good leg I had tried to hold. Seeing the Levi jacket over his face made me remember all the things I had meant to buy him and give him, sometime or other. I had meant to buy him a blanket-lined jacket, for one thing.

I heard a whiz. Hud's arm swung. There was a whistle, and the whiskey bottle hit the ground somewhere in the pasture. "Whiskey, ain't it," Hud said. His voice wasn't loud. I saw there were still grass burrs in Granddad's legs. In a minute I felt Hud come and stand behind me. I couldn't feel any of Granddad there with us; it

158

was just Hud and me. I looked up at him and he was looking off into the dark. I felt like I would gag again, but inside I was all dry and hot, like I had fever. Hud was looking into the pickup headlights, stretching his hands out toward them like the lights were a fire and it was winter.

"Lonnie," he said. "No shit, it was the best thing. The pore old worn-out bastard."

"But he woulda been," I said. "It woulda been all right, he woulda got well. I needed him." I started to pull the jacket off and look at Granddad's face, but I didn't. Hud came around in front of me and squatted down. I knew he wanted me to listen to him. He looked right at me, and didn't do it to scare. I saw sweat on his cheeks, but his voice seemed easy for once, not mean or rough.

"You listen to me," he said. "No shit, it was best. I ain't lyin' now. Homer wanted it."

"But he wasn't so bad," I said. That was all I could say. If I could have felt Granddad was there, I could have felt something to say. But it was just Hud and me.

"Hell, I had to," he said. "He was bad off, Lonnie. You wasn't here. You wasn't acoming, and he got to spittin' blood and tryin' to get up, an' hurtin' himself. Tryin' to get to them goddamn dead people a his. I thought if he wanted to get to 'em so bad I'd just let him go. He always liked them better than us that was alive, anyhow."

"But he was Granddad," I said.

"He was all fucked up," Hud said. "He was throwin' up blood, and that leg like it was. Worse than it was the first time he hurt it. He was just an old worn-out bastard. He couldn't a made it up no way in the world. He couldn't a made it another hour."

Then Lily come over an' hung on Hud's shoulders, mumbling something about Truman in his ear. But he didn't even look around at her; he was still talking to me.

"But what will I do?" I said. "Granddad was always . . ."

"You'll do without, like the rest of us," he said. "Lonnie, no shit

159

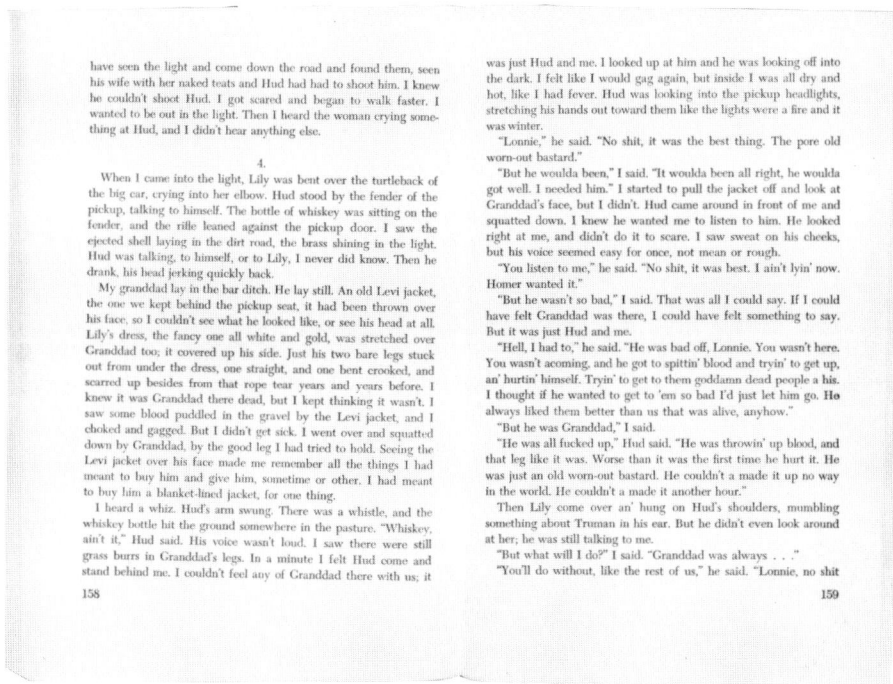

3. McMurtry continued to rewrite the crucial murder scene during the fall at Stanford. In the published version, he has removed some of the profane edge from Hud's speech and replaced it with hints of fear and indecision. The result is new insight into Hud's character, suggesting how deeply ambivalent were his feelings about his stepfather.

Ironically, as he rewrote the book to satisfy Leggett, McMurtry himself became increasingly dissatisfied, convinced that he had been pushed into unnecessary changes. Just after the publication of Horseman, Pass By in the summer of 1961, McMurtry wrote to Wallace Stegner, "I ran it through one too many drafts. I think if I had quit it about the time I got to Stanford, instead of about December, it would have been all to the good." Years later McMurtry summarized his thoughts about Leggett's role: "After a certain amount of argument, a young writer is particularly vulnerable to an intelligent editor. You tend to think, well, he knows better than I know. Eventually I gave in."

N. Scott Momaday

In poetry, fiction, and memoirs, N. Scott Momaday fuses the oral traditions of the Native American past with the avant-garde techniques of modernism. These radically different aesthetics intersect for Momaday in their shared assumption of the imagination's power to transfigure reality through language. For both, speech is originative, capable of projecting worlds of numinous order where individuals can dream themselves fully into existence. "We are what we imagine," Momaday explains, adding that "man has consummate being in language, and there only." Sustained by this doubly grounded faith in words, Momaday recreates the values of his American Indian heritage in a contemporary idiom that is unique to modern letters.

Momaday is a Kiowa, born in Oklahoma in 1934 and raised by parents who were deeply committed to their ethnic legacy. Al Momaday was a widely respected artist whose work captures the ceremonial splendor of Plains Indian customs, and Natachee Scott Momaday self-consciously reconstructed her Cherokee origins and celebrated them in both books and paintings. Though the Momaday homestead is located near Rainy Mountain in the Wichita Range of Oklahoma, Momaday spent most of his childhood on the Navajo reservation in Arizona and his adolescence at the Jemez Pueblo in New Mexico. His serious interest in writing developed when he was an undergraduate at the University of New Mexico, where he took a political science degree in 1958. The following year, while teaching on the Jicarilla reservation, Momaday was awarded a Stegner Fellowship to study poetry with Yvor Winters at Stanford. In the summer of 1959 the two met, and a close friendship developed, continuing until Winters's death in 1968. During that period Momaday completed his doctorate in English and began an academic career that eventually brought him back to Stanford as a faculty member from 1972 to 1980. Today he lives in Tucson and is Regents Professor of English at the University of Arizona.

Momaday started his writing life as a poet. His first published poem, "Earth and I Gave You Turquoise," is a haunting elegy for a Navajo woman that he composed the year before coming to Stanford. Its diction is charged with allusions to Navajo customs and landscape, while its syntax beautifully evokes the rhythmic flow of the tribe's ritual chants. Once under Winters's tutelage, Momaday schooled himself in the techniques of formal English verse and addressed more traditional literary themes, which he treated in a highly concentrated, often oblique manner. A major achievement of this period is the title poem of his first collection, *Angle of Geese and Other Poems* (1974), a volume that gathers many of the poems written under Winters's influence during the 1960s. "Angle of Geese" itself is another elegy rooted in Momaday's reservation memories. But here, a philosophical meditation on death displaces his earlier narration of personal feeling. Supporting this more abstract approach is a new stylistic sophistication, evident in his subtle use of the syllabic line that Winters personally advocated. Such technical virtuosity continues to inform Momaday's poetry, even though since the 1970s he has distanced himself from Winters's aesthetic and returned to looser forms and Native American subjects. Among the most impressive signs of this later phase is the title sequence of his second collection of poetry, *The Gourd Dancer* (1976). A tribute to Mammedaty, his Kiowa grandfather, the suite focuses on crucial episodes in Mammedaty's life, projecting them vividly into the present. Momaday's act of historical imagination casts his Kiowa imagery into formal and free verse patterns that register the cadences of his ancestor's oral culture.

This repossession of his Indian heritage in the idiom of contemporary literature is at the very heart of Momaday's artistic ambitions. Toward the end of his student days at Stanford he started the work that evolved into the Pulitzer Prize-winning novel, *House Made of Dawn* (1968). Set in Jemez and drawing on Momaday's memory of pueblo life and his knowledge of Navajo customs, the book dramatizes the identity crisis suffered by a young Jemez Indian coming to manhood during World War II. The novel documents Abel's alienation, beginning with his disaffection from the tradition-bound ways of the Indian community and charting the further erosion of his Native American culture in conflict with the white world. Thematically, Momaday acknowledges the inevitability of the social forces that threaten the survival of Native American civilization, and he unsentimentally rejects nostalgia for pre-Anglo America. Instead he emphasizes the need to preserve Indian values by reimagining them in the context of the present. This difficult challenge *House Made of Dawn* triumphantly meets through its own style, which uses the devices of modernist fiction to express the spiritual legacy of the aboriginal Southwest. In Momaday's art, such contemporary techniques as collage, stream-of-consciousness, paratactic syntax, and mythic structure all serve a classic Indian vision, in which space and time, spirit and matter, humanity and nature merge into a sacramental universe of beneficent wholeness.

Momaday's next book, *The Way to Rainy Mountain* (1969), is devoted to his own Kiowa heritage and reflects a deep desire to establish personal bonds with his tribal background. Momaday had grown up removed from the homeland of the Kiowas, whose civilization was, in effect, destroyed more than fifty years before his birth. But a pilgrimage in 1963 to Oklahoma to see the Kiowa's sacred Tai-me bundle and then a visit to his grandparents' graves at Rainy Mountain made Momaday realize that an important part of himself remained unexplored and inarticulate. Commenting on this encounter with his ancestral past, Momaday explains, "I could sense in that situation the vitality in myself, I could sense it but could not take possession of it until I had translated it into language. Language is not an aid at all, but an essence." *The Way to Rainy Mountain* performs that essential act of translation. It condenses years of painstaking research into a highly original, rhetorically resonant structure, recording the emergence, triumph, and decline of the Kiowa people. Each of the book's twenty-four brief chapters contains a triad of paragraphs that treat a single event from the mythic, the historical, and the personal perspective. The effect is to bring the Kiowa legacy powerfully to life, by simultaneously reasserting the timelessness of its legends, incarnating them into the process of history, and then moving them forward into our own immediate world.

Momaday's most recent book, *The Names* (1976), continues to examine his own heritage but shifts the focus from tribe to family. Tracing the forces that shaped his identity, the memoir lovingly recounts the lives of relatives, both remote and close, including remarkable portraits of his parents. It also rehearses the formative events of his childhood, recreating the images that imprinted themselves indelibly on his consciousness and gave direction to his artistic aspirations. But Momaday's clearest signature here is not the content of this personal saga but its language, which moves with astonishing suppleness and energy. Perhaps more completely than ever before in his career, Momaday has adapted the methods of high modernism to his own cultural agenda. The result is that *The Names* not only recalls many recent masterpieces of English prose but also shifts the canon of twentieth-century literature, making room for a new voice that speaks with equal sophistication but in a profoundly different accent.

I admire writing that is concentrated and well made. A poem, by definition, is such a kind of writing. I admire especially poems that grow out of ancient oral traditions of singing and storytelling. The first songs and stories that I heard were sung and told to me by my father, from the Kiowa. When I was a child I lived among the Navajo and Pueblo peoples, and their oral traditions became very important to me. Later I spent time among the Uzbek and Tagic peoples of Soviet Central Asia and the Eskimos of Alaska, the Northwest Territories, and Greenland. The oral traditions I found in these places reinforced the one into which I was born. I hope and trust that some of the qualities which inform these old institutions of language inform my own writing.

The traditional forms of poetry in English represent other institutions of language, and of these I knew relatively little when I came to Stanford as a Creative Writing Fellow in 1959. From Yvor Winters I learned how to construct a poem according to the rules of prosody. That learning was and is very important to me. Much of what I have written in the last twenty-five years has been determined in some measure by what I learned in the poetry workshop, which in my day was led by Winters in his office on the English corner. "In some measure" in the foregoing sentence is perhaps a fortunate pun. "Measure" is a key word, for it is what distinguishes poetry from other kinds of expression. Measure was very much on our minds—the four or five of us who sat around the table—in those days. Winters admonished us to write little and write well. I have lived with this admonition for a long time now. It remains among my best examples of good advice.

N. Scott Momaday

Selected Works by N. Scott Momaday

Fiction

House Made of Dawn. New York: Harper & Row, 1968.

Poetry

Angle of Geese and Other Poems. Boston: Godine, 1974.
The Gourd Dancer. New York: Harper & Row, 1976.

Other

The Way to Rainy Mountain. Albuquerque: University of New Mexico Press, 1969.
Colorado: Summer, Fall, Winter, Spring, photographs by David Muench. Chicago: Rand McNally, 1973.
The Names: A Memoir. New York: Harper & Row, 1976.

Editor, *The Complete Poems of Frederick Goddard Tuckerman.* New York: Oxford University Press, 1965.

Individual Interview

"N. Scott Momaday: Literature and the Native Writer," with Tom King. *Melus,* Winter 1983.

1. *Yvor Winters's tutelage of N. Scott Momaday continued well after Momaday had completed his doctorate in 1963 under Winters's supervision and left Stanford. In this letter, written during Momaday's tenure on the faculty of the University of California at Santa Barbara, Winters remains securely in his professorial role, even assigning a reading schedule. The Momaday poem he discusses is "Angle of Geese," which was published three years later in the* New Mexico Quarterly *and subsequently used as the title piece in Momaday's first book of verse,* Angle of Geese and Other Poems *(1974). Momaday did, in fact, follow Winters's counsel and change the article to the indefinite.*

April 12, 1965
143 West Portola Ave.
Los Altos, Calif.

Dear Scott:

       Thanks for the poem. It is even finer than I remembered. But I suggest one small change for ultimate book publication: in the second line of the last stanza change the to a. This will make it perfectly certain that you are referring to the fact that the goose is looking at the disappearing flock, not the poet or the hypothetical bystander. The associational (but clear) relationship of the second half of the poem to the first half is precisely the relationship that you will find in many of the odes of Horace: look at the first four or five of Book I, for example. I tell you this just in case anyone should ever object to your procedure. In fact the relationship is often less clear in Horace. Horace is the only one of the Latin poets whom I read many years ago to whom I ever return. At his best he is a great poet. I have a very good bilingual text published by G.P. Putnam's Sons in 1929, the English translations (prose) by C.E. Bennett. The odes and epodes in one volume (these are what you should read) and the satires and epistles in another (some of these are important in the history of critical theory, but for this you could read the English). You ought to work your way through one of the shorter odes each week, to improve your Latin. With the help of the English on the opposite page it would not take much time.

       If your library has a classical journal called Arion, published at the University of Texas, you ought to look into it. It is now in its third volume. I subscribe to it and pass it on to Dan as I finish. Read the statement of principles in I-1, and then follow Arrowsmith especially through later issues. They are waging war on academicx stupidity. When I was young, the departments of English were very much like the departments of classics which they describe: seedy descendents of German philology. Now we have too little scholarship of any kind and too much amateur criticism. But the lack of intelligence and the fear of intelligent men remains the same.

Yvor

1.

Headdress, Red-tailed Hawk

Wherefore this medicine of flight:
The feathers raddle the loose hair,
The wings collect and craze the light
And conjure fire from the dark air.

2.

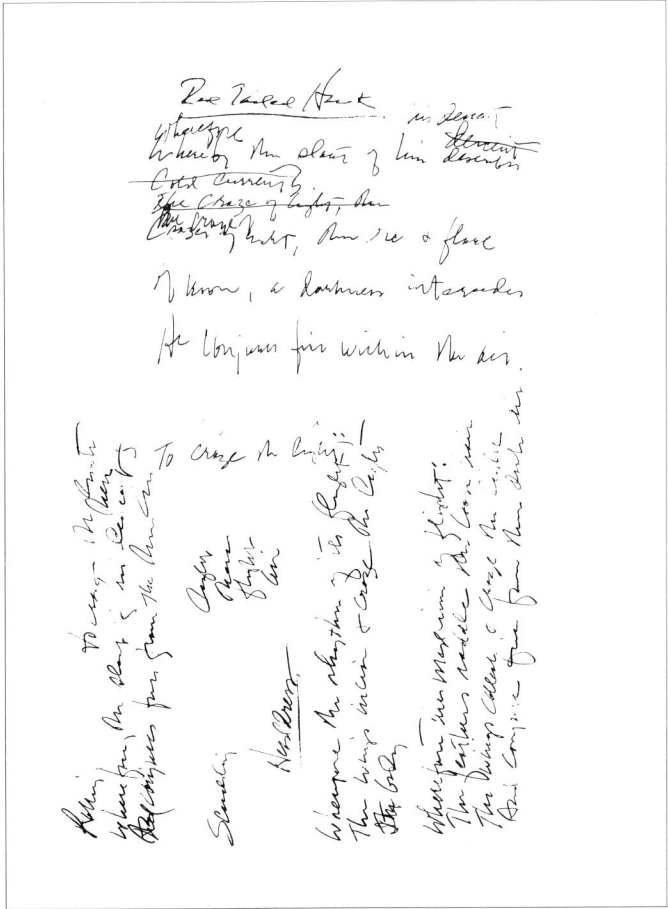

3.

2. Momaday's poetry moves confidently among a variety of forms, sometimes employing rhyme and meter in conventional stanzaic patterns, on other occasions working in looser syllabic and free verse rhythms. In "Headdress, Red-tailed Hawk," a recent unpublished piece, Momaday uses a tightly structured iambic quatrain to capture the magical interpenetration of nature, spirit, and humanity in native American ritual. Momaday's ballpoint pen drawing on the late typescript draft of the poem is similar in style to the sketches he made to illustrate several poems in his second volume of verse, The Gourd Dancer (1976). Since the mid-1970s, painting and drawing have become increasingly important outlets for Momaday's creative energy. His growing reputation as a visual artist has, in fact, earned his work numerous solo shows and museum exhibitions.

3. "Headdress, Red-tailed Hawk" began as a poem about the beauty of a hawk in flight. The initial manuscript draft is called "Red-tailed Hawk" and runs across the top of this page. It shows Momaday working quickly in a series of phrases, each occupying its own line. The poem's second, untitled version, written vertically in the lower left-hand corner, refines the visual impression of the bird's descent through the bright sky. Immediately underneath is the third draft, which introduces the new title word, "Headdress." This final manuscript draft at first maintains the poem's original focus on the bird, beginning "Wherefore the rhythm of its flight." But after three lines, Momaday breaks off and entirely reconceives the quatrain, now writing, "Wherefore this medicine of flight." The term "medicine" refers narrowly to the feathers of the headdress and more broadly to the native American belief in the efficacy of such ritual objects to "conjure" nature's powers. This religious concept underlies Momaday's poetic strategy, which fuses hawk and headdress into a single image united by the spiritual energy of a ceremonial dance.

N. Scott Momaday 61

Tillie Olsen

At the 1988 Modern Language Association conference a special session commemorated the tenth anniversary of *Silences*, Tillie Olsen's revolutionary work of literary scholarship. *Silences* uses a collage of biography, criticism, and quotations to document the political, financial, and personal pressures that force writers into artistic silence. "The silences I speak of here," Olsen says, "are unnatural: the unnatural thwarting of what struggles to come into being, but cannot." Her book not only examines suppressed creativity among recognized writers; it also reveals that silence is the dominant condition of our culture. Economic imperatives, social isolation, and lack of education block self-expression for the greater part of the population. And beyond these practical hindrances, Olsen suggests, there exist more subtle emotional and psychological barriers. She shows how class, color, sex, and the temper of the times destroy for most people the "conviction as to the importance of what one has to say, one's right to say it." Thus the profoundest and most painful silence is that of ordinary individuals who never write because their confidence and creativity have been stifled.

Although the authority of *Silences* derives partly from the breadth of Olsen's reading and the insight of her commentary, it arises mainly from Olsen's experience of having her own artistic energies "consumed in the hard, everday essential work of maintaining human life." She explains, "I have had special need to learn all I could of this over the years, myself so nearly remaining mute and having to let writing die over and over again in me."

Tillie Olsen was born in Nebraska in 1912 or 1913. Her parents were Russian immigrants who had participated in the 1905 democratic upheavals against the Czar and fled from the threat of greater oppression. While Olsen was growing up in Omaha, her father became the state secretary of the Socialist Party, and she was exposed early to the local world of socialist politics, where people labored six days a week and attended meetings at night. In her home, Olsen read magazines like *The Comrade* and *The Masses* and studied the Little Blue Books that the publisher Haldenman-Julius designed for self-tutoring workers. Olsen was also an avid patron of the public library and qualified herself for academic high school, which she attended until her senior year and where she first learned about class differences. After leaving school, Olsen worked as a trimmer in a slaughterhouse, a power-press operator, a hash slinger, a mayonnaise-jar capper in a food processing plant, and a checker in a warehouse. At the same time she committed herself politically, joining the Young Communist League at eighteen and trying to organize Kansas City packing house workers at the beginning of the Depression. In 1933, when Olsen was twenty, she moved to California. The following year she was arrested and imprisoned for supporting the unions during the San Francisco General Strike. Throughout this period Olsen balanced jobs and political involvement with the raising of her children, dedicating what little time was left to the pursuit of writing.

In March of 1932 she had begun a novel that followed a migrant family through the twenties and the early years of the Depression as they moved from a Wyoming coal-mining town to a South Dakota tenant farm and then to the slaughterhouses of an unnamed city. In 1934 an early chapter of this book appeared in *Partisan Review*, and the editors of the newly established Random House offered Olsen a monthly stipend to finish the novel. The demands upon her time and energy, however, were so intense that by 1937 she abandoned the novel and set aside any hope of completing even the shortest works of fiction. In "snatches of time I wrote what I did in those years, but there came a time when this triple life was no longer possible," Olsen says. "The fifteen hours of daily realities became too much distraction for the writing. I lost craziness of endurance."

For the next twenty years, while Olsen raised four daughters and labored at routine jobs—most often as a secretary—"the simplest circumstances for creation did not exist." But in 1955 at the age of forty-two, while still working full time, she took an evening course in creative writing at San Francisco State University. The next year, on the basis of a draft of the story "I Stand Here Ironing," she won a Stegner Fellowship. On her arrival at Stanford in the fall of 1956, Olsen experienced a freedom that she had never known before in her adult life. "I had continuity," she remarks, "three full days, sometimes more—and it was in those months I made the mysterious turn and became a writing writer." Indeed, it was while at Stanford that Olsen completed three stories and began the fourth that together became her first published collection, *Tell Me a Riddle* (1961).

The stories in *Tell Me a Riddle* revolve around three generations of a family. They are told from different points of view and in strikingly different voices. Ranging in perspective from that of a working mother to that of a San Francisco sailor, from that of an old Russian immigrant woman to that of a young white girl at a black Baptist church service, the stories weave intricate patterns of memory and emotion. They describe the shared experiences of tragedy, humor, and hope that unite individuals otherwise separated by differences of culture, religion, and age. Stylistically, Olsen reinforces her theme of the diversity of our common humanity by endowing each story with a language wholly its own. Grammar, rhythm, narrative style, and idiom shift dynamically to represent the rich heritage of American English. By giving voice to speech patterns that normally go unheard in our society, Olsen introduces her readers to ways of living that are at once foreign, familiar, and irrepressibly alive.

After the publication of *Tell Me a Riddle*, whose title novella won the O. Henry Award for the best short story of 1961, Olsen was a Fellow at the Radcliffe Institute for Independent Study (1962-64) and a recipient of a grant from the National Endowment for the Arts (1967). In the late 1960s she then began a series of visiting professorships which took her to Amherst College, the Massachusetts Institute of Technology, and the University of Massachusetts as well as back to Stanford. While at Radcliffe, Olsen started a project that reflects her commitment to recovering forgotten but important books. When she was fifteen, she bought in an Omaha junk shop several *Atlantic Monthly* issues from 1861, which contained an anonymous work of fiction titled "Life in the Iron Mills." For years Olsen tried to discover the author's identity but only in 1958 did she learn that it was Rebecca Harding Davis. After reading extensively about Davis during her stay at Radcliffe, Olsen began teaching the nineteenth-century novel in her own classes. In 1972, when the Feminist Press republished Davis's work, Olsen provided a long afterword, which helped restore the book to its rightful place in American letters.

That same year, while searching through old papers of her own, Olsen rediscovered pages of the novel she had begun forty years earlier at the age of nineteen. A more thorough search turned up other parts of the manuscript, and after piecing the fragments together—without adding any new writing—Olsen published it in 1974 as *Yonnondio: From the Thirties*. Here she probes the American system of life and liberty, showing "what a criminal system this was, and what this did to human beings." On the surface, the story is a struggle for physical survival, as the Holbrook family contends with hazardous working conditions, near starvation, and bitter cold. Against this backdrop Olsen reveals the deeper drama of the human spirit and its fight against extinction in the vast machine of American capitalism. Amid the emptiness and despair that almost overwhelm the characters' lives, Olsen's compassionate art captures moments of courage and imagination that affirm what she calls the "phoenix rebirth of the human spirit."

This is about sources, wellsprings, and the enabling gift of circumstances in the eight temporal, infinite, Stanford months when I "made the mysterious turn and became a writing writer." And something of these accompanying scraps, notings, mss. pages.

I did not come to our writing class that late September day in 1955 as the others came. I was a quarter of a century older. I had had no college. I came from that common everyday work, mother, eight-hour-daily job, survival (and yes, activist) world seldom the substance of literature.

I came heavy freighted with a lifetime of ever-accumulating material, the sense of unwritten lives which cried to be written. I came from a twenty-year silence "when the simplest circumstances for creation did not exist.... Nevertheless there was conscious storing, snatched reading, beginnings of writing, and always the secret rootlets of reconnaissance."

I came as stranger; of the excluded. I came as the exiled homesick come home—*my* home, where literature, writers, writing had centrality, had being. I came to Dick and Ann Scowcroft, the Mirrielees sisters, my to-be first and dearest writer friend, Hannah Green; to the hovering presence of Stegner (then on leave), and to unnamed others who embodied that centrality—and remain living sustenance to this day.

I came to circumstanced time.

We met two afternoons a week in the Jones Room, around an oval, an egg-shaped table (shape of new life in creation) encircled by walls solid with books. A writer's library, carefully gleaned, gathered together as if to concentrate for us, incite to, what makes our medium incomparable. The imperishable, the good, side by side with letters, lives, journals of their creators—illuminating, intertwining, the ways of their begetting, the joys...labor of their creation.

Encircled, bulwarked so, we practiced writing companionship: read what we had written, listened to each other, talked writing, vivified. Or so it was for me. Enormous had been my morning—with books and notebook in the library, or with the Jones Room books; enormous and yielding would be my late afternoon and evening for I would stay until the last train. When it was possible, I rode from home (San Francisco) with my new friend, Hannah Green, and for the first time had occasion to read aloud, hear in my ears, sounds, rhythms, silences of the written. I read what I had long loved or just come to love: from Verga's *Little Tales of Sicily* to which Hannah had introduced me; all of Cather's "Wagner Matinee," Glaspell's "Jury of Her Peers," Chekhov's "Gusev," "Rothschild's Fiddle," "Ward #6"—among other treasures. And I was in a frenzy, a passion, of starved intense reading, copying; observing, noting, putting together; re-remembering; *writing*—in this vast strange freedom of wholly my-own time.

In those circumstanced months, in that writing air, the comradeship of books and writing human beings, in that freed time (for all that there was still full family life, responsibilities)—in contrast to the years it took for the writing of "I Stand Here Ironing", the first "Hey Sailor, What Ship?"—I came to facility. I made "Hey Sailor" publishable. I wrote all of "O Yes." I began, finished, the first third of "Tell Me A Riddle." Although I did not know it then, I was also gathering, even writing, what would later become substance and actual page after page of *Silences* ("this book was not written, it was harvested")—and comprehensions, lines, paragraphs in other work accomplished the years since.

1955-56. Profound earthquake years, presage years—for me; for my country, for our world (therefore also for me). Forty-three years old then, born in 1912 or 1913, I had lived through such periods before, but only now had I time to try to comprehend them, record their impress as they occurred, even try to shape into literature. As I tried in "O Yes", "Tell Me A Riddle." 1955-56: Year of writing resurrection for me—yet year of arterial closeness to death and dyings of four of the human beings ineradicably dearest to me: my mother, my father-in-law Avrum, Seevya, and Genya (whose last days of dying are inscribed in "Tell Me A Riddle"). All four of that

great vanishing generation whose vision, legacy of belief—in one human race, in infinite human potentiality which never yet had had circumstances to blossom, in the ever-recurring movement of humanity against what degrades and maims—I tried to embed in that novella.

Year for me of overwhelming realization—death-occasioned—of the vulnerability and transience and dearness of life. World year of escalating nuclear threat—and seeming defeat for the petition movement of millions the earth over to totally disarm; only Picasso's peace dove, created as symbol for us, seemingly remaining.

1955-56: Presage year indeed for our country. Year that began still in the McCarthyite shadow of fear; of pervasive cynical belief that actions with others against wrong were personally suspect, would only end in more grievous wrong; year of proclamation that the young were a "silent generation," future "organization men."

Year of the Supreme Court decision against segregation "which generates feelings of inferiority"; of Rosa Parks, Birmingham, Little Rock. Year of the first happenings of freedom movements, movements against wrong, which were to convulse and mark our nation and involve numberless individual lives.

So was burgeoned "O Yes" ("Baptism"). So was begun "Tell Me A Riddle." (Both sourced in the years before as well.)

Other wellsprings fed:
I was again migrating from one world into another—and in more than the twice-a-week commute to Stanford. It had been so with me, unarticulated, in my youthhood, when I crossed the tracks to Omaha's academic high school. It was so now with me, as it was happening in my children's lives. I was freshly experiencing, re-experiencing that terrible agony, harm, of having to live in a class/sex/race separating, circumscribed time, when those among whom we are born, live, work, those with whom we are most deeply bonded, cannot journey along with us into that other world of books, of more enabling circumstances for use, development of their innate capacities.

I was living more and more, too, in the world of written language (some of it consummately used), (though the sound of written language, spoken aloud in class, read to Hannah, my own words spoken to myself while writing, was coming often into my ears).

For years, for nearly a lifetime, in love, in wonder, in envy, I had noted, kept evidence of the *other* consummate way language is, has been used: the older, more universal oral/aural —by "ordinary" human beings denied the written form. On scraps, in notes, in memory—and now, in my Stanford time, typed up, garnered together: remarkable phrasings, expressions, song lines, wisdoms, characterizations heard, spoken, sometimes sung, by unwritten, unwriting others in my life.

I had circumstanced time. I had profoundest need—to encompass, make tangible, visible (I hoped indelible) all the above. So did "O Yes" come to be. So was begun, and one-third finished, "Tell Me A Riddle."

Then—had to return back to that uncircumstanced world of what silences.

Tillie Olsen

Selected Works by Tillie Olsen

Fiction

Tell Me a Riddle. Philadelphia: Lippincott, 1961.
Yonnondio: From the Thirties. New York: Delacorte Press, 1974.

Other

Silences. New York: Delacorte Press, 1980.
Mothers and Daughters. New York: Aperture, 1987.

Editor, *Mother to Daughter, Daughter to Mother.* Old Westbury: Feminist Press, 1984.

```
sharks     dragons  los bandidos   the gents   royal esquires   warlords   aces   templars
Apaches    Barts  Road runners   Shieks

he hurted me so bad    all my good feeling days is gone
  I done worked & worried & slaved & raised him & he should write

looks like an accident goin somewhere to happenth

they lives in the old plush

get myself conglomerated

write him a bawlen out letter

sick of this sluggin & tuggin & worryin
                 dug up   drug up   beatoun & wore out
fire wagons       slaughter pan

I dont fly fly when they say shoo shoo   I got stubborn wings
he like to collapse
its all I kin do is work  not work & worry both

my dumb brat background  ntohing to brag off at all
m ake all kinds of oaths & swears
the natural truth
she scorch up some

I dont want that boy to just make a livin   I want him to do some livin

all those testes
               nothing to brag off at all
I'm tellin you the true
nearly killed me graveyard dead

she runnen me crazy      feel like somebody tromping my heart
wear myself to death
just got me down in the dumphouse
in the middle of a bad fix
rhey definly said it
he shoots off to everybody   the policemans   why cant something be did about it
  "I'll blow you in"   they stomped him in the head   jab it off   hes on the needle see
he abrused me    overrejoiced
thats a boy and  a half
the mens out of work    just saing it to pass off   thats about the size
mamma you maulin me
I'M LOOKED DOWN ON   what czn be did about it
loafin his time down
clothes done gone
rthoughin it through
a hippy dip

         that is what she do
         we tired of everybody frontin us off
         the policemans
         a real mannerable boy
         get their licks in
         we not animals   we peeple
         that wasnt right
```

1.

Until Tillie Olsen was in her mid-forties, the demands of daily life forced her to pursue her art in improvised and fragmentary ways. Because time was so scarce, only quick jottings and brief sketches on cards and in pocket-sized notebooks were possible. These writing habits continued even after a Stegner Fellowship gave Olsen the leisure to develop her ideas more fully. Looking back over the papers and manuscripts surviving from the year at Stanford, Olsen comments: "Little remains of the makings of what came to publication. Here are samplings of the scraps and pages that remain of the loosenings, the wellings just as they came, the practicing of freedom which perhaps made the facility possible; the rounding out and completion of a thought, a story kernel, a noting—where before could only be one word, a scrawl of line, in thieved minutes—to leave some deposit, to affirm that there still lived in me a writer being."

1. Caught in the press of family obligations and without the money to buy books, Olsen got into the practice of copying quotations from library books onto 3x5 cards. These, she explains, "I could carry with me for available moments to re-read, ponder, or learn by heart. Yes they have come stained over the years, dog-eared, torn—tacked (as still they sometimes are) over sink or stove during tasks, or over my work desk, or still habitually pulled out to re-read while on the bus or waiting somewhere."

In addition to transcribing quotations from canonical authors, Olsen also carefully compiles "evidence of the…way language is, has been used" by America's different cultural groups. Her sensitivity to different modes of speech is evident here on a large blue sheet that records the distinctive words and syntax of black San Francisco diction. This material, gathered together from years of jottings, is integral to the story "O Yes," which is set in a black Baptist church and reflects Olsen's special interest in strains of American English which for racial and class reasons are often excluded from the written medium. Her respect for the integrity of diverse ethnic voices signals the democracy of Olsen's art, which celebrates diversity within its unifying vision of human community.

2. Olsen's techniques for revising are as precise and scrupulous as the note-taking she does before starting to write. Exemplifying these methods is the evolution of "Requa I," which originally appeared in the Iowa Review and then in the Best American Short Stories of 1971. The story is about a recently orphaned San Francisco boy who moves to the northern California town of Requa to live with his uncle, Wes. In this early typescript Olsen edits single words to sharpen her rendition of the boy's view of the junkyard where his uncle works. In the bottom left-hand margin, next to the typed list of the tools and parts the boy sees, Olsen also pencils in other possibilities such as coils, sprockets, bits, and braces. Later, she checks off each word as she includes it in the next draft. The different-colored pen and pencil marks covering the page suggest that she has revised it no less than four times.

2.

3. After incorporating the editorial changes from the preceding version into a fresh typescript, Olsen continues to revise "Requa I." Each corner of this page contains marginal notations that suggest new words or different avenues to pursue in later drafts. The note at the bottom entitled "Rifts" is a provisional outline for a major new section that will eventually treat in detail each of the junkyard images listed—lathe, breadbox, clothes shed, rags, and rotting harness. Also important at this stage is Olsen's concern for line-by-line layout, especially different indentations and the underlining of sentences for italicization. In the galley proofs Olsen continues to pay strict attention to layout, seeking a visual appearance that corresponds to the intricate play of her prose style.

3a.

3b.

Robert Pinsky

"The poem, new or old," Robert Pinsky observes, "should be able to help us, if only to help us by delivering the relief that something has been understood, or even seen, well." This faith in the clarifying power of poetry governs Pinsky's work both as poet and as critic. In *The Situation of Poetry* (1976) he elaborates his belief in the capacity of the rational imagination to identify and illuminate the problems that confront contemporary Americans. There he counters modernism's radically nominalist bias by urging a revival in verse of a discursive language which reaches beyond the immediacy of particulars to generalized statements about experience. Pinsky's reassertion of poetry's historical role as an instrument of intellection does not, however, carry a specific program of ideas. Indeed, for Pinsky, the artist's responsibility is not to legislate, but to liberate. Aesthetic form, he explains in his recent collection of essays, *Poetry and the World* (1988), "expresses the craving to be free of imposed, controlling abstractions. It is a made, bodily abstraction to challenge the abstractions of circumstance." This is exactly the challenge to which Pinsky's own poetry responds. His work isolates with uncanny accuracy those commonplace notions around which we unconsciously organize our lives and submits them to intense scrutiny. By exposing the limitations and contradictions of the cultural concepts that define us, his poems open our understanding onto new mental spaces and help set us free.

Born in 1940, Robert Pinsky grew up in the small town of Long Branch, New Jersey, a declining ocean resort where his family had lived for two generations. Like his parents, aunts, uncles, cousins, brother and sister, Pinsky graduated from Long Branch High School. During his freshman year at Rutgers, his adolescent interest in music gave way to a growing fascination with literature and writing. At the university he majored in English and edited the student literary magazine. As a senior, Pinsky married Ellen Bailey, now his wife for nearly thirty years. Her decision to transfer to Stanford prompted Pinsky's own application to the doctoral program in English, which brought him to campus in the fall of 1962 and shortly afterwards into Yvor Winters's circle. "Most of my graduate education consisted of reading English and American poetry with Winters," Pinsky says, adding that the rigors of that encounter rescued him from "blithe anti-intellectualism."

During this Stanford period Pinsky spent one year as a Stegner Fellow in poetry under Winters and also saw his first poems reach print in national magazines. It was not Winters, however, but another Stanford professor, Albert Guerard, who encouraged Pinsky to take the Romantic poet Walter Savage Landor as the subject of a doctoral dissertation that he completed in 1966. Two years later that study became *Landor's Poetry*, Pinsky's first published book. By then he had already launched his academic career, which took him briefly to the University of Chicago before longer periods on the faculties of Wellesley College and the University of California at Berkeley. Today Pinsky teaches at Boston University.

Not until a decade after Pinsky's poems began appearing in prominent literary magazines did he gather them into his first collection, *Sadness and Happiness* (1975). The volume includes many short occasional pieces, ranging in subject matter from elegiac recollections of Pinsky's New Jersey youth to a witty allegory about the strokes and strategy of tennis. Uniting such diversity is Pinsky's intellect, which persistently seizes and subverts the easy clichés that are the currency of our personal lives. The wisdom of prudence, the virtue of charity, the mind's desire for order—all of these commonplaces Pinsky's poems rigorously test, exposing the complex alloy of meanings within their apparent simplicity.

This same critical impulse achieves fuller expression in the book's two long sequences. "Essay on Psychiatrists" is a meditation on contemporary psychiatry as metaphor and symptom of the human condition. The poem's fretful search for "healing speech" comes to figure Pinsky's own artistic quest for a language precise enough to cope with our universal "sense of contingency and confusion." This quest is also pursued in the volume's title poem, "Sadness and Happiness," which analyzes those two self-evident ideas, disclosing the ambiguous exchange of meanings between them as well as among such other cherished abstractions as life, death, nature, and art. The poem's concluding movement catches this complicated conceptual interplay and illustrates Pinsky's singular ability to endow generalizations with the density of sensuous imagery: "art and life/both inconstant mothers, in whose/fixed cold bosoms we lie fixed,/desperate to devise anything, any/sadness or happiness, only/to escape the clasped coffinworm/truth of eternal art or marmoreal/infinite nature...."

In his next book, *An Explanation of America* (1979), Pinsky shifts attention to the public, political sphere. Begun in the mid-1970s during the disillusioned aftermath of Vietnam and Watergate, this single long poem is addressed to Pinsky's daughter and self-consciously shoulders the burden of making optimistic sense of the nation for the child. "I want our country," he says to her, "like a common dream/To be between us." To accomplish this redemptive project and envision a sane, habitable America, Pinsky must challenge, he explains in an interview, all those "comfortable or fashionable responses and tones in myself—both complacencies *and* cynicisms that might be easy, too automatic." The poem consequently rehearses a whole repertory of clichés about America—the country's absolute uniqueness, its freedom from the past, its romance with progress, its successful "denial of limit," and looming grimly above these conventional ideas, Malcolm X's image of the republic as a prison house. To test such emotionally charged myths, Pinsky assembles a marvelously disparate body of evidence, including the behavior of Brownie troop leaders, Hannibal's siege of Saguntum, Horace's epistle on goodness, and a production of Shakespeare's *The Winter's Tale*. Once examined within this larger scope of human culture and feeling, America's stock truths gradually lose their tyrannical grip on consciousness. No longer seen as infallible, they become instead useful signs of our local American circumstance, together forming a legacy of explanation that Pinsky can bequeath to his daughter.

Pinsky's newest book of poetry, *History of My Heart* (1984), returns to the personal lyrics of *Sadness and Happiness* while retaining the broad cultural perspective of *Explanation of America*. This series of powerful poems unites the emotional intensity of autobiography with profound intimations of human destiny. Here Pinsky is most concerned to forge generalizations that sensitively connect particulars with universals. This drive is clearly present in the book's opening poem, "The Figured Wheel," which accumulates an astonishing range of detail around the unifying image of the wheel of fate, with all of creation ultimately "figured and prefigured in the nothing-transfiguring wheel." Though disturbing in its totalizing vision, the poem, like many others in *History of My Heart*, has a dimension of ironic exuberance. This tone recalls Pinsky's other work of 1984—an electronic novel about a world teetering on the edge of destruction. Centered on a different kind of wheel, one of wisdom, not fate, *Mindwheel* is structured so that the readers themselves determine the narrative's outcome. Though a surprising departure from past work, this computer game nonetheless draws on the same qualities that animate Pinsky's poetry and criticism and render them such a valuable cultural asset— "my ability to play around, to live with uncertainty and the possibility of failure," as well as, he adds, "my capacity to experiment in an optimistic muddle."

The writing program as "program" didn't really exist at Stanford in those days. My writing life at Stanford was dominated by two presences: Yvor Winters was one. The second was a remarkable group of fellow students.

There's a slightly distorted recreation of Winters (as "The Old Man") in Section XX of my poem "Essay on Psychiatrists." Oddly enough, those lines are based less on my memory of Winters than on a little riff about Winters I heard Bob Hass do at a party—I was much closer to Winters, saw more of him than Bob did. This odd bit of pickpocketing on my part may be partly a tribute to Hass's memory and anecdotal gift, partly a comment on the peculiarities of memory.

Winters was a tyrant. He bullied students, read aloud to them from his published essays, ridiculed opposing points of view, attempted to indoctrinate students by pouring his learning and opinions into them as though they were empty vessels. Anyway, he was a great teacher: inspiring, powerful, utterly serious, a model of intellectual integrity and passion. He taught me so much, and I resisted him so hard, that some part of me still resists and learns. (Winters also is a gorgeous, passionate lyric poet, underestimated by criticism and in my opinion misunderstood by his disciples—the "Wintersians," as they were called.) He once assured me that Sonny Liston was going to make mincemeat of the young boxer then known as Cassius Clay; I picked Clay. After the fight, Winters told me, "All the experts were wrong: I am an expert." Another time, he complained about getting old. I pointed out that he was only a few years older than Cary Grant. He said, "Who is Cary Grant?" He also claimed not to know who Cole Porter was. I don't know if he was putting me on.

As to the students, many of my contemporaries went on to publish impressive books. My closest friends in this category are Robert Hass, James McMichael and John Peck. (I knew John Matthias only slightly, and saw Ken Fields mainly in classes.) We were not part of a *writing program*: the student poets were defined not by Stanford, but by how much they had to do with Winters. This ranged from a lot of direct contact (Peck, Fields) to a kind of removed, attentive opposition (Hass).

An interesting fact about those of us who went on to publish books of poems is that unlike many Stanford graduate students we had not attended famous or "distinguished" colleges: no Harvard, no Amherst, in fact, no Stanford. Hass came from St. Mary's College in Moraga, Peck from Allegheny College in Pennsylvania, McMichael from the University of California at Santa Barbara. Whatever other significance this fact may have, I think it did constitute a personal bond.

In the time of the Free Speech Movement and early protest against the American involvement in Vietnam, some of us founded an organization called the Graduate Co-ordinating Committee. The GCC published a lively newsletter, edited by Hass. The first issue contained a movie review by the editor, memorably entitled "Coming Out of Mother." Also a bad poem by me, about Nazi concentration camps. This poem resulted in Swastikas being painted on my house—by fraternity boys, I have always thought—an incident that thrilled us all.

I wish I had more colorful memories. Albert Guerard was a wonderful supporter of literary and progressive graduate students, a kind of buffer between us and Stanford stuffiness. There was a graduate student softball game; McMichael was such a good athlete that he threw things off for the rest of us. David Thorburn wrote a parody of Winters' essays on Jones Very and others, called "The Works of Smith Extremely." For this work I wrote all of Smith Extremely's poems: a sonnet, a two-line epigram, a villanelle, and so forth, all with the same paraphrasable content. I can remember only the couplet, which was modeled on a quite wonderful American eighteenth-century one Winters admired, which goes something like,

I now repose my weary head upon
My pillow, but I shall be shortly gone—

quite good, really—so Smith Extremely wrote:

> I now insert a seedless roll into
> My lunchbox, but I shall be
> shortly through.

I remember that the sonnet elaborated on lunchbox, that it had Mickey Mouse on it, etc. This seemed immensely funny at the time. I think we showed the poems and essay to Al Guerard, who chuckled and advised against sharing the joke with Winters. I think all copies are gone.

I left Stanford for London in May of 1965, after three years. At the time, Bruce Franklin was a scholarly young Wintersian, not yet a fiery radical. Donald Davie had not arrived. Winters was alive. When a college friend of mine was arrested for activities registering Black voters in Alabama, I posted on the English Department bulletin board an appeal for donations toward legal fees, channeled through an organization called the Student Non-Violent Co-ordinating Committee. Winters wrote the only check that came in. (As I recall, the two objects displayed on his office walls were a picture of Herman Melville and a citation from the NAACP.) Litton Savings in downtown Palo Alto, in honor of the American space program, gave away little foil pouches of Space Food, desiccated beef and vegetables that found their way into graduate students' stews. Palo Alto was sleepy and unsophisticated, very much a genteel white Protestant's town. Stanford still was The Farm, but starting to change. At Berkeley, the right-wing Young Americans for Freedom had joined the Socialists in demanding free speech and advocacy in Sproul Plaza. The Stanford chapter of S.D.S., resistant to old-fashioned ideologies and rhetorics, was founded. Within a year or so, everything was different. Yvor Winters died on January 25, 1968: in retrospect, a kind of dividing line.

Robert Pinsky

Selected Works by Robert Pinsky

Poetry

Sadness and Happiness. Princeton: Princeton University Press, 1975.
An Explanation of America. Princeton: Princeton University Press, 1979.
History of My Heart. New York: Ecco Press, 1984.

Other

Landor's Poetry. Chicago: University of Chicago Press, 1968.
The Situation of Poetry: Contemporary Poetry and Its Traditions. Princeton: Princeton University Press, 1976.
Mindwheel. San Rafael: Broderbond Software, 1984.
Poetry and the World. New York: Ecco Press, 1988.

Translator, with Robert Hass, *The Separate Notebooks*, by Czeslaw Milosz. New York: Ecco Press, 1984.

Individual Interview

"An Interview with Robert Pinsky," with Mark Halliday. *Ploughshares*, 6.2, (1980).

1. Robert Pinsky's "Pilgrimage," a recent, uncollected poem, began its complex evolution as a contemporary rewriting of Psalm 139. Its earliest, untitled typescript, which Pinsky labels with the Roman numeral I, concentrates on the Hebrew song itself, casting it into the voice of a single priest. A later typescript, titled "Psalm 139," also emphasizes the Biblical text but imbeds it in an outdoor religious ceremony that culminates with the worshipers' joining the priest in song. The fifth stanza of this draft elaborates a waterfall image from the first version, transforming it into a symbol of the divine spirit with which the celebrants seek ecstatic union. The pantheistic deity invoked in Pinsky's poem contrasts sharply with the jealous, authoritarian patriarch addressed by the Old Testament psalmist.

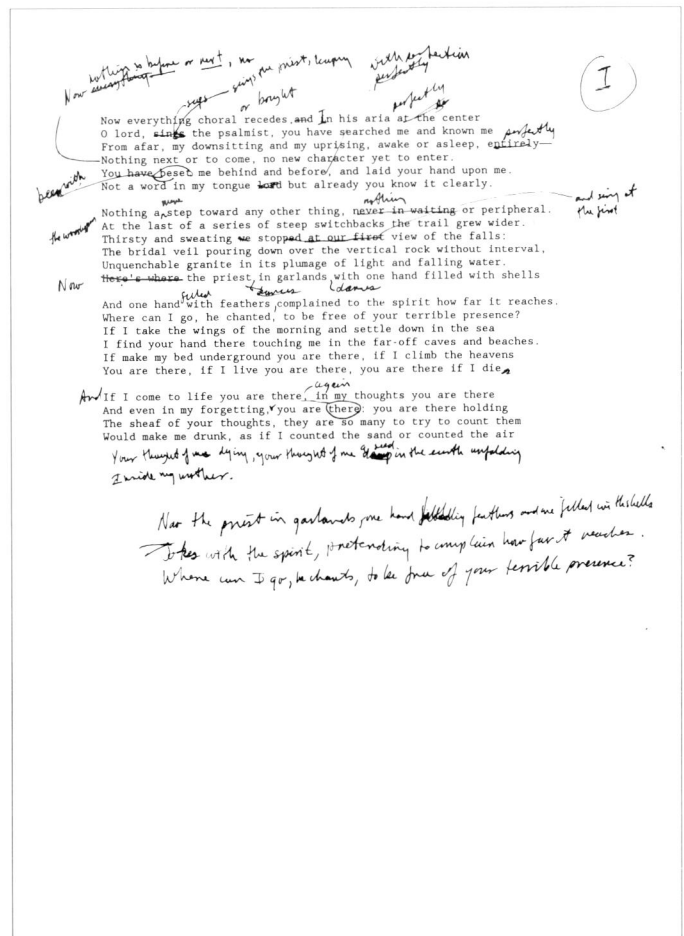

1.

2. Numerous drafts intervene before this late typescript, which incorporates the first appearance of the poem's eventual title, "Pilgrimage." Formally, this version abandons the leisurely six-line stanzas used in the earliest drafts and adopts short-lined triplets that accelerate the poem's forward movement. Thematically, Pinsky increases attention to the scene and spectacle of ceremony. The most important changes in this version occur on the second page. First, Pinsky deletes "illusion," substituting the term, "vision," to describe the worshipers' religious experience. This crucial shift in diction collapses the emotional distance between the poet's voice and the celebrants' ecstasy. Pinsky's elimination of irony at this point anticipates his other major change, a completely new conclusion. Here he successfully merges the psalm, the scroll's sacred text, the waterfall, the participants, and the poem itself into a single aesthetic whole that formally celebrates the mystical union enacted by the ritual.

3. The final version of "Pilgrimage" shifts from fixed-length stanzas to organically variable divisions, each marking a unit of thought, event, or feeling in the poem's dramatic development. Pinsky's other major revision in this draft is adding five lines that intensify the mystery of the celebrants' secret names. These appear on the second page, ending, "And behind each unutterable name/The name of that name's/Name in infinite regress." Inserted just before the conclusion, the passage reduplicates that sense of the infinite resident in the finite which the waterfall has already come to represent. The effect is to lend greater resonance to the poem's spiritual union of nature and humanity.

Now nothing is next or before, there is
Nothing yet to enter, you have beset me
Behind and before, you have put

Your hand upon me, though I am
Fearfully and wonderfully made,
You have known me from afar.

Now for many of them
The falls seem motionless: hung
From the foamless brim in an illusion

Of suspended flowing, falling
But unfallen. Through tears
of pleasure they squint upward. Now

When they take the thick weazened scroll
Out from the arc in its white armor
and unfurl the crowned letters

Scorched and stained into the skin
In a catalogue of names—Alfease, Deoru,
Tennefille, Nathrong—they read themselves

Into the unchangable book of the journey
Begun before your body was made,
Before you were a seed packed in honey, before you

Fell from the brim, fashioned and torn
From the cold water that tumbles
Forever down the face of the mountain.

2.

PILGRIMAGE

Near the peak. A clear morning,
Camphorous air of eucalyptus and mountain laurel
Lining the steep trail.

They chant in chorus as they climb,
Some of them in turns bearing
The ark—its hammered silver
Ornaments jangling, the pressure
Of polished cedar beams heavily
Afloat on their shoulders,
The others reaching in
To touch it as they dance and kiss
Their fingers that brushed it.

At the last of the dusty switchbacks
The trail grows wider and flatter
And they pause, flushed and shuffling.
They lower the ark to the earth,
A priest singing his aria
From beside it: Now I call you by your
True name—and they come forward:

One by one he fits
Embroidered blinders over their eyes
And guiding them singly by the hand
Singing the secret name of each
He leads them from the ark upward
To the cliff's edge, till the whole choir
Stands dancing in place
At the precipice, each man and woman
Chanting in a darkness.

At the prayer's end
They lift the blinders
To see the falls across the sheer vacancy:

Mountain light, the bridal veil
Skimming the great vertical
Rockface without interval,
Unquenchable granite in its plumage
Of air and falling water:
                        O Presence
You have searched me and seen me from afar,
My downsitting and my uprising.
Now nothing is next or before, there is
Nothing yet to enter, you have beset me
Behind and before, you have put
Your hand upon me, though I am
Fearfully and wonderfully made,
You have known me from afar.

3.

Alan Shapiro

"Without a living sense of the past, we can only be prey to fashion," Alan Shapiro remarks in "The New Formalism," his defense of the historic commitment of English poets to metrical verse. Countering proponents of free verse who condemn contemporary usage of traditional poetic forms as reactionary and repressive, Shapiro argues that the older metrical techniques open expressive possibilities otherwise closed to today's writers. But the revival of past practice that he advocates entails no rejection of present methods. "It's dangerous," he insists, "to think we have to choose exclusively between free verse and form." Indeed, for Shapiro, the choice of literary technique is a matter not of cultural politics but of instrumentality. Its single purpose is "to bring the widest, most unrestricted play of mind and heart to bear upon the widest range of life." Precisely this ambition animates Shapiro's own poetry, which adopts conventional as well as experimental modes to explore the psychological drama of human life, both past and present.

Born in Boston in 1952, Shapiro grew up in one of the city's tightly knit Jewish neighborhoods. During his undergraduate years at Brandeis, he developed a strong interest in Seamus Heaney's poetry, prompting him to spend a year in Ireland after graduation. It was while he was living in Dublin that Shapiro was awarded a Stegner Fellowship in poetry, which brought him to Stanford in 1975. After his fellowship year, he taught creative writing at Stanford for three years as a Jones Lecturer, before accepting an appointment to the faculty of Northwestern University, where he is now a professor of English.

Shapiro's first volume of poetry, *After the Digging* (1981), is a haunting act of historical imagination that explores human behavior at the extremities of physical and emotional distress. Consisting of two parallel suites of dramatic monologues, the book opens with a sequence spoken by witnesses of the catastrophic famine that plagued Ireland between 1846 and 1849. The poems imitate nineteenth-century documents, including an official memorandum and letters, a newspaper story, and entries from a ship's log. The writers are mostly Englishmen and thus outsiders to the horrors they observe. Though speaking with bureaucratic formality, they feel anguished sympathy for Irish suffering, a tension between style and content sustained by Shapiro's adroit handling of blank verse. The contrast between the speakers' restrained manner and their intense emotion creates an eerie atmosphere of helpless fatality.

Shapiro sustains this sense of doom, with a twist, in the second suite of poems. Here he reaches back to an even earlier epoch and recreates the pathology of religious fanaticism in seventeenth-century Puritan America. In this section the poems emerge directly from the consciousness of the victims. Perhaps most impressive is "Hands of Compassionate Women," an extraordinary rendering of a public confession by a woman whose tormented guilt at the love she bears her daughter drives her to drown the child. It ends:

> But I have come to tell you, you good people,
> that when I heard her small weight hit, her one
> brief cry, I felt—as you may never feel—
> that what He hath intended hath been done,
> and praised Him for the light He took away,
> and praised Him because I knew at last, that I
> was damned, and that the dark was comforting.

Shapiro's remarkable stylistic control and subtle irony channel the sensationalism of this event into a rigorously ethical perspective, casting an unnerving light on the perversion of human values under intense pyschological pressure.

Shapiro's interest in dramatic situations that reveal deeply conflicted feelings also informs his second book, *The Courtesy* (1983). Here, however, the subject matter is essentially autobiographical, and the personal voice carefully effaced from *After the Digging* predominates. The volume is arranged thematically in two sections. The first part, "The Storm," draws on Shapiro's childhood memories of family and neighborhood to project an emotionally turbulent world shaped by the strictures of Jewish culture. Sentiment and nostalgia play artfully throughout this section, but its governing tone is pained alienation. This emerges powerfully in several poems about paternal authority. "Perfect Son" chillingly juxtaposes the father's "aloof and unappeasable" assertion of "sheer law" with the son's desperate need to convert his "unworthiness" into love. "Simon, the Barber," the book's most widely praised poem, uses the prejudices of an old Jewish barber against the young to extend the theme of paternal authority into the irreconcilable differences that divide generations.

"Crossing" is the title of *The Courtesy* 's second part, where Shapiro shifts his focus to adulthood's "elusive sadnesses, fugitive regrets." In a world of abandoned apartments and morning headaches, the hallmark word is "distance," which echoes through poem after poem, signifying those psychological spaces that separate people from each other as well as from themselves. Often the distances that Shapiro charts arise from the loss of intimacy. Characteristic is "Harvesting," a California poem that bleakly contrasts nature's fullness with an impoverished romance:

> And though it's winter and in the garden now
> the lemons hang like worlds, forever day
> for someone else, what weighed on other boughs
> we harvest separately, and take away.

The habit of emotional restraint bred by such failures is a condition Shapiro also examines. Particularly remarkable is the book's concluding poem, "The Names." Dedicated to his Stanford teacher, Kenneth Fields, and Fields's wife, Nora, it beautifully catches Shapiro's unease at his own reserve, begging his "Dear Friends" to "forgive the good distance of my tact."

Happy Hour (1987), Shapiro's most recent collection, intensifies his vision of the contradictory impulses that complicate our lives and confound our personal relations. The book's title poem presents a harrowing view of a couple bound joylessly together in a ritualized exchange of bitterness and guilt, while "Familiar Story" captures the empty, sometimes cynical conventions of sexual courtship. These are typical of *Happy Hour* 's lyrics, individually focused on moments of crisis or revelation but collectively forming a parable of love's problematic fate in contemporary urban America. The narrative drive that underlies Shapiro's shorter poems emerges fully in the book's long centerpiece, "Neighbors." This blank verse tale of a psychotic neighbor and the impact of her sinister behavior on a young couple differs from Shapiro's typical approach, for here the irrationality that threatens happiness is an outside force. But as the story unfolds, the interplay between characters becomes so intricate that the neighbor's slide into madness seems to foreshadow the couple's own prospective fate. Shapiro follows this tale of psychic dislocation with a small group of poems dramatizing the angers and fears of childhood. These add new and darker dimensions to the portrayal of his youth that begins in *The Courtesy* and join with the rest of *Happy Hour* to confirm the growing authority of Shapiro's representation of middle-class America. His is a painfully recognizable picture, where desire and circumstance perpetually conflict. But countering the "familiar story" of living "restless, and remote, and unforgiving" is Shapiro's highly controlled style. Constantly declaring a more generous consciousness, it redeems despair and transfigures the daily round of losses into hope.

When I came to the Stanford Creative Writing Program in 1975, most American poetry was committed to one kind or another of free verse lyric, and most poets and critics of poetry assumed that formal verse was old-fashioned and mechanical, incapable of responding to the urgencies of the contemporary world. Poets as different as Allen Ginsberg, Robert Duncan, Galway Kinnell and Robert Bly (to name only a few of the poets popular during the seventies) insisted that only free verse and its improvised rhythms could render faithfully the contours of immediate experience, and that the business of the poet was not to traffic in ideas or statements but to present and juxtapose images and feelings with as much concreteness and intensity as possible. During my Stegner year I studied with Ken Fields and Donald Davie. Despite the many differences between them as teachers and poets, they both shared a powerful distrust of the exclusive thinking which the new orthodoxy demanded. The value of form, they never tired of saying, whether free or traditional, open or closed, depends entirely on what one manages to say by means of it, and it is therefore just as possible to write with passion and surprise in tight measures as it is to write predictably in loose ones. More importantly, they encouraged us to go against the grain of our inclinations and habits—to write in meter and rhyme if all we'd ever written was in free verse; to read Oppen or Dorn, Pound, Bunting or Ronald Johnson if all we'd ever read were Winters or Cunningham. In a true spirit of experimentation, they encouraged us to try to integrate, not choose between, what literary fashion told us should be kept apart. Only in such an atmosphere of intellectual and aesthetic generosity could I have had the confidence to try my hand at the historical narratives which comprise *After The Digging* and at the same time to write the free and formal lyrics of *The Courtesy*. Moreover, because Davie and Fields were scholars as well as poets, one didn't feel any sort of tension or division between the academic and creative disciplines. Creative writing wasn't segregated from the scholarly community. And this proved enormously helpful when I was writing poems about the late 17th century New England Puritans. I felt no compunction in asking Jay Fliegleman, a professor of American Literature, either for advice in researching original documents or for criticism on the historical accuracy of the poems I eventually wrote. In fact, it was through Jay that I obtained microfilm of the sermons which Samuel Parris delivered in Salem Village during the witchcraft hysteria, sermons which inform directly or indirectly the suite of poems called "Captivities" in *After The Digging*. Finally, what I learned from the Stanford Writing Program, and what I hope the poems I've gone on to write embody, is the flexibility of mind that refuses to be guided in its choice of form, style or subject by anything but curiosity, intelligence and passion.

Alan Shapiro

Selected Works by Alan Shapiro

Poetry

After the Digging. Chicago: Elpenor Books, 1981.
The Courtesy. Chicago: University of Chicago Press, 1983.
Happy Hour. Chicago: University of Chicago Press, 1987.

Alan Shapiro wrote After the Digging (1981) while he was at Stanford, first as a Stegner Fellow and then as a Jones Lecturer in the years 1975-1979. The book's title refers to the burial of the victims of Ireland's diastrous potato famine, and is drawn from the volume's opening suite, which explores the tragedy of that event. Shapiro conceived the idea for these historical poems during the year he spent in Ireland just before coming to Stanford. After the Digging's other section, called "Captivities," focuses on Puritan New England. The extensive library research underlying both these imaginative recreations of the past was also done at Stanford and is clearly reflected in the two notebooks that Shapiro used while drafting the poems that make up the collection.

1. The Irish segment of After the Digging concludes with "Passage Out," a long poem that adopts the format of a ship's log book to recount the physical and emotional horrors suffered by Irish emigrants on a voyage to Canada in 1847. In the published version, there are entries for nine different days over the weeks from June 1 through August 10, but in the early manuscript drafts Shapiro is not yet organizing the sequence by date. His intense, compacted method of composition is especially evident in the notebook, where he opens a new passage with the line, "Ship fever breaks out and spreads." On this and the next three pages, Shapiro reworks his initial line six more times. At first he uses the phrase like an invocation, to impel his attention into the passage; then he recasts the line by introducing a simile and temporarily settles on "Quick as a prairie fire, ship fever has broken out." Eventually this line is changed yet again to "Ship fever, faster than fire,/has broken out" and the entire passage condensed into the poem's twelve-line entry for June 20.

1.

2. "Hands of Compassionate Women," the first poem in the "Captivities" section of After the Digging, originated for Shapiro with a single paragraph from the August 1637 entry in John Winthrop's Journal. Elaborating Winthrop's spare account of a spiritually distraught woman who drowns her own child, Shapiro boldly imagines her first-person confession. The draft begins tentatively on the left-hand page, with the woman addressing her congregation, "Good neighbors, do not wonder at me now/that I am calm as the wick of a flame." To heighten the poem's rhetorical impact, Shapiro withholds both here and in the final published version one fact from Winthrop's report—that unknown to the woman, neighbors have saved the child.

At the top of the facing page Shapiro inscribes the phrase, "Refuse Silver," as if it were the poem's title, and then proceeds to quote Jeremiah 6:30, the passage where it occurs. In its original context, the image symbolizes those people whose evil is beyond redemption, a group to which the poem's speaker appears to belong. Later Shapiro drops this material, instead citing as his epigraph Lamentations 4:10, in which innocent children suffer for their parents' iniquity.

3. Two more fragmentary pages intervene between the provisional opening of "Hands of Compassionate Women" and this fuller version, which is written in black felt pen and begins, "Good neighbors, as you look upon me now/you seem angry to see me, who has been so much a trouble to you." The draft moves forward smoothly for a page before breaking off. Later, Shapiro returns to it, working with a blue ball point pen. He now focuses on the woman's reference to hope and spends an entire page writing over and over a single line until it becomes the passage, "My hope, like an erratic exaltation/of larks…" This effort to render the language more vividly reflective of the speaker's consciousness also occurs on the notebook's next two pages, where Shapiro concentrates on the woman's concept of goodness, an exercise from which only the word "palsied" survives in the final version. Here, as throughout these notebooks, Shapiro uses the page the way a painter handles a canvas, treating it as a literal scene of creation, where the physical act of writing, including random doodling, is an integral element of the process of composition.

2.

3.

Scott Turow

In 1986 after Scott Turow finished *Presumed Innocent,* Farrar Straus Giroux had so much confidence in its popular appeal that the company advanced Turow the largest sum ever authorized in its history for a first novel. When Turow's suspenseful courtroom drama appeared in 1987, this confidence proved justified. The book was critically acclaimed and spent eleven months on the hard-cover best-seller lists. This remarkable reception was no accident of the publishing industry but was hard-earned, springing from Turow's long dedication to the craft of fiction and his knowledge of the American legal system.

Scott Turow was born in Chicago in 1949. After receiving his bachelor's degree from Amherst College in 1970, he was awarded a fellowship by Stanford's Creative Writing Center for study towards a master's in English. Here he participated in the fiction workshops and published several stories, two of which were cited for distinction in the 1971 and 1972 volumes of *Best American Short Stories.* After finishing the course work for his degree in 1972, Turow remained at Stanford another three years as a Jones Lecturer. But while he devoted himself to his writing during these years, Turow also grew dissatisfied with his distance from the quotidian world outside the academy. "When I was a young writer, sitting at my typewriter every day," he says, "the isolation, in the sense that I was feasting on experience I was trying to imagine, just didn't cut it for me." Turow wanted his writing to reflect his life rather than replace it. So in 1975 he decided that the writing of fiction "would have to be a private passion" and left Stanford for Harvard to pursue a longstanding fascination with the law.

During his first year in law school, Turow continued to refine his craft by keeping a detailed diary of his experiences. This personal account, published in 1977 as *One L,* traces the emotional, moral, and intellectual changes that he underwent at Harvard during his arduous initiation into the world of law. As Turow comments in the preface, "It is during the first year that you learn to read a case, to frame a legal argument, to distinguish between seemingly indistinguishable ideas; then that you begin to absorb the mysterious language of the law." Ten years later, *One L* is still in print and has become a virtual textbook of survival for first-year law students across the country.

In 1978 when Turow graduated from Harvard Law School at twenty-nine, he returned to his native Chicago to become a prosecutor for the United States Attorney's office. He stayed there for eight years before joining the law firm of Sonnenschein Carlin Nath & Rosenthal, where he is now a partner. Late in his career as a federal prosecutor Turow received sudden notoriety for his involvement in "Operation Greylord," a highly publicized series of trials that exposed judicial corruption. As a prosecutor, Turow helped convict members of the bar and numerous public officials, including the Attorney General of Illinois, for various offenses, among which were conflicts of interest, bribery, and tax evasion. During these trials Turow learned that "if the criminal justice system is supposed to be a truth-finding device it's an awkward one at best," and this observation inspired Turow to explore "the different kinds of truth we recognize" through the medium of fiction. Starting with the image of a murdered woman, Turow began piecing together the story of violence, corruption, and duplicity that was to become *Presumed Innocent.*

The novel opens with the death of Carolyn Polhemus, a member of the Kindle County prosecuting attorney's staff. As Rusty Sabich, the deputy prosecutor, begins to investigate his colleague's murder, he uncovers an intricate network of corruption and deceit extending throughout the county's judicial system. "Absolutely everybody in the novel is guilty of something," says Turow. "That's a truth of life that I learned as a prosecutor." Indeed, guilt eventually marks each of the central characters, including Sabich, the novel's narrator. The mystery of Polhemus's death is an engaging narrative, but it also provides the context for Turow's examination of the subtleties of legal procedure and how they both incorporate and reflect the pervasive deceit of human psychology:

> It is a given of the criminal justice system, an axiom as certain as the laws of gravity, that defendants rarely tell the truth. Cops and prosecutors, defense lawyers and judges—everybody knows they lie. They lie solemnly; with sweaty palms and shifty eyes; or, more often, with a look of schoolboy innocence and in incensed disbelief when their credulity is assailed. They lie to protect themselves; they lie to protect their friends. They lie for the fun of it, or because that is the way they have always been. They lie....

Throughout the novel, Turow probes the complex interplay between truth and appearance, between language and lies, that exists both in the legal system and in the art of fiction. "We talk about literary truths as implausible, fictitious," Turow says, "and yet there's a way in which the mystery novel delivers a truth that real life can't deliver. Often you get that in a trial: the jury says not guilty, and you don't know who did do it." It is this insight that makes *Presumed Innocent* a demanding novel, one that transcends its genre. As Anne Rice comments in the *New York Times Book Review, "Presumed Innocent* is without a doubt an ambitious and absorbing novel, the work of a profoundly gifted writer with a fine, distinctive voice."

While I was at Stanford, I learned what I always treated in my own mind as The First Rule and First Corollary of storytelling. They are embarrassingly simple ideas, but they were somehow news to me.

Both are based on a quotation of Chekhov's. The phrase was often repeated by Wally Stegner and Nancy Packer, but I can no longer remember it exactly, and I apologize to them, and anyone else who has a better memory for quotations. To paraphrase, then: If there is a gun hanging on the wall in the first act, there must be a shooting in the third. Or perhaps I have it reversed: If there is a shooting in the third act, a gun must be hanging on the wall in the first. In any order, these are the principles I refer to.

Whether as rule or corollary, these notions were revolutionary to me, because they articulated concepts I had never quite understood. I soon appreciated, however, that they were inevitably correct. All plot, I believe, is based fundamentally on this idea, that the action must be an enlargement upon what we already know about the characters and their circumstances; and obversely, that no action, after we have made a character's acquaintance, will win our belief if it does not grow out of what the audience has already learned. Finally, a rule of authorial economics is implied: no major action should be included if it does not have later consequence.

I found myself deeply satisfied by a universe that moved to these rules. As a writer, I have always favored plot—big, sinewy stories, with lots of dips and turns. I like surprises and reversals—mostly because that is the way I am made, but also because I believe that is the way everybody else is made, too. The form of stories is often similar around the world. I think that is because our knowledge of one another is roughly the same. Plot, in the sense Chekhov defined it, shows us what life so often does as well: that character is fate, that the past is the future, that the unexpected is only the less expected.

In writing *Presumed Innocent* I tried to keep these principles in mind. I wrote for nearly two years without knowing the end of my would-be murder mystery; when I started I had a vague idea that the killer would never be caught, and I surprised myself as I found the narrator dropping clues about his own culpability. Finally, after two years' writing, and about one hundred twenty pages of manuscript, I took two years away from the book to figure out the turns and inversions. In doing this, I looked to the Chekhov-Stegner-Packer principles for guidance, and tried to figure out what action naturally arose from the characters and events I had thus far chosen for myself. Eventually, much of the denouement came to me, and when I started writing again, I drafted the end.

Ultimately, in the summer of 1986, I took three months away from law practice to finish my novel. The plot was well worked out in my own mind, but this was the first time I had ever gone through the book from start to finish. Oddly, to me, the book always had two halves: before and after Rusty Sabich's accusation. When I finished, I was surprised to find that my first "half" was no better than a third of the manuscript. But, as Chekhov taught, it was there that all the real work of establishing the plot was going to be done.

Scott Turow

Selected Works by Scott Turow

Fiction

Presumed Innocent. New York: Farrar
Straus Giroux, 1987.

Other

One L. New York: Putnam, 1977.

Individual Interview

"Scott Turow," with William Goldstein.
Publishers Weekly, 10 July 1987.

*Scott Turow began developing the story
for* Presumed Innocent *(1987) shortly
after he started working for the United
States Attorney's office in Chicago in
1978. He spent two years writing notes to
himself in longhand in spiral notebooks
while riding to work on a commuter train
and another two years thinking about the
novel's plot and structure. During this
time, he also wrote a novella that interested Jonathan Galassi, executive editor of
Farrar Straus Giroux. This initiated a relationship that culminated a few years later,
when Galassi published* Presumed
Innocent.

*1. After elaborating the details of the nov-
el's plot, Turow sat down to write. "At
that point," he says, "the precise order of
events became important, and that I had
to work out on paper. That is the origin of
these few sheets where the sequence of
chapters is sketched. The cryptic one- and
two-word notes—e.g. 'Barbara,'
'Carokid'—refer, as often as not, to the file
names of my computer discs. My word
processing program will not accept a file
name longer than eight characters, so I
was required to be fairly terse. These
papers reflect one subplot about a jail-
house informant....By the end of the summer, I recognized that much of that material could be worked into the Chapter I
called 'Prjects' (for Projects) which
remains pretty easily identifiable in the
completed book. The chapter order here
varies slightly from what ultimately
appeared in* Presumed Innocent *because
one chapter called 'Carolyn' was ultimately divided, at the suggestion of my editor,
Jonathan Galassi, into three and inserted
rhythmically throughout the book's first
section. Material on Nico Della
Guardia—the new 'Ch 6'—was later
moved 100 pages further on."*

1a.

1b.

Tobias Wolff

Tobias Wolff's fiction shuns today's fashionable aesthetic of purely formal experimentation. The arts in America, he observes, have a "general preoccupation with method at the expense of their interest in the human," and "literature is in danger of becoming similarly stylized and self-absorbed." Wolff rejects such artistic self-consciousness because it fails to articulate the crises of contemporary culture. "We live in a great silence," he says, "where what frightens us and moves us and sustains us is rarely given voice." In his judgment, the avant-garde techniques of modern fiction are "simply another form of silence." To counter this tendency, Wolff reasserts traditional realism, adapting its conventions to the task of representing American reality. Through precise detail and dialogue, he diverts our attention from narrative method and draws us steadily into the realm of everday action, until modernism's structures of silence begin to collapse. "When that silence is broken," says Wolff, "we bend forward and listen."

Born in 1945 in Birmingham, Alabama, Wolff grew up among natural storytellers, including his father, the notorious con artist Duke Wolff, and his older brother, novelist Geoffrey Wolff. Tobias Wolff continues in the family line. "I think and remember in terms of stories," he explains, tracing the habit to his childhood: "I honestly remember writing stories when I was about six years old." Wolff pursued his interest in fiction throughout a painful youth and adolescence, a period he recreates in his newly issued memoir, *This Boy's Life* (1989). Then in 1964, at eighteen, he joined the U.S. Army Special Forces and served in Vietnam from 1967 to 1968, leaving the service with the rank of first lieutenant. Upon discharge he went to England, where he took a first in English at Oxford University. There he also began to write fiction again, and on the basis of drafts of two novels Wolff was awarded a Stegner Fellowship in 1975. Once at Stanford he shifted his focus to the short story. "When I try to work in longer forms," Wolff says, "I feel like I'm beating them into existence. I feel a kind of clumsiness…[but] writing stories feels more natural to me. Maybe it's because it's closer to the act of telling stories, and that's something I've always done."

After leaving Stanford, Wolff taught literature and writing at a number of universities, eventually joining the faculty of Syracuse University in 1980, where he has remained ever since. At Syracuse, Wolff consolidated several of his Stanford stories with new material and published them in 1981 as *In the Garden of North American Martyrs*. The book opens with the story, "Next Door":

> Next door the man is still yelling, but I can't make
> out what he's saying over the dog and the baby.
> The woman laughs, not really meaning it, "Ha! Ha!
> Ha!," and suddenly gives a sharp little cry.
> Everything goes quiet.
> "He struck her," my wife says. "I felt it just the same
> as if he struck me."

This passage captures the lucidity and care for detail that distinguish Wolff's fiction. Rather than using elaborate stylistic devices to mediate his narrative, Wolff presents his story directly. He renders the movements and sounds so vividly that the action seems to be taking place just across the street. The transparency of Wolff's language rivets our attention to the story's violence and loneliness, luring us so deeply into its events that when everything goes quiet, we feel as if we, too, have been struck.

Although *In the Garden of North American Martyrs* was well received by some critics, it was not widely reviewed. Only in 1984 when Wolff's short novel, *The Barracks Thief*, won the P.E.N./Faulkner Award for that year's best work of fiction, did he achieve national recognition. The manuscript was originally several hundred pages long, but, Wolff explains, "I whittled and carved and sculpted that bulk of verbiage…down to its least components, down to the most exact possible statement of the situation." What remains is a powerful story of masculine comradery, sexuality, and violence. It follows three men who meet in training camp before shipping out to Vietnam. Lewis, the central character, is plagued by a sense of inadequacy. Driven by a desire to prove his manhood, he visits a prostitute, but to pay for her constant services must steal from the other enlisted men, betraying those he had wished to impress. When Lewis is discovered, the company's first sergeant forces him to confront a friend he has robbed:

> "Look at him," the first sergeant said again. He
> pushed Lewis's chin up until Lewis was face to face
> with Hubbard. They stood that way for a time.
> Then…Lewis gave a soft cry and covered his face
> with his hands.

Wolff's hard-hitting immediacy draws us down into the story's dark currents of sexuality and violence, forcing us to confront our own obsessions face to face. Under the spell of Wolff's art, imaginative participation reawakens us to our contemporary world.

Many of Wolff's characters struggle with failure, either in jobs, in private relationships, or in personal ideals. They are, he says, "people who aren't what they dreamed they would be, and aren't what they still wish they were." But Wolff does not indulge in "that easy cynicism that so many writers display as a sign of their sophistication." Instead, he uses the occasion of the failed dream to uncover opportunities for human connection that normally go unnoticed. The stories in Wolff's latest collection, *Back in the World*, (1985), exemplify this pattern. The book's characters are trapped in the routine of everyday life. But when they come into contact with strangers, they find themselves liberated from habit and convention. Buried emotions, convictions, and confidences rise to the surface, and, suddenly, the characters are able to renew communication with lovers or friends. In "Coming Attractions," a lonely young woman cannot relate to her family. Her father lives in another state, her mother divides her time between dating and work, and her brother can barely hear her over the blaring television. She holds her own feelings at bay with sarcasm. But one night, while making a crank phone call, she finds herself drawn into conversation. She can hear the inexplicable sympathy in the voice of the old man at the other end of the line, and her cynicism begins to give way under this single exchange of emotional concern.

The optimism of this story is not merely thematic. It also arises from Wolff's belief in the affirmative qualities of writing itself. In his eyes, the imaginative exchange between writer and reader is a commitment to open communication and an embrace of the possibility of change. Storytelling, says Wolff, "assumes community, shared lives with a shared perception of the world. It goes against the grain of cynicism and pessimism…the very act of being a writer seems to me to be an optimistic act."

On "Coming Attractions"

My stories all come to life in different ways. A line of music can set one stirring, or an image—three soldiers in a mud-spattered jeep on the coast highway—or a memory suddenly breaking surface after years in the depths. Sometimes I draw from life. "Coming Attractions" is, in a manner, drawn from life; but it is also a complete fabrication.

We had a rough kid living down the street from us, a girl, bony and mean-looking, maybe thirteen years old. I used to watch her go by with her little brother and their unleashed, savage German shepherd. She walked with a hard, jolting stride, and stared fiercely ahead, holding her brother's hand in a grip that made my own hand ache. They were said to be responsible for all the bent radio antennas in the neighborhood.

One day the boy came by alone. He was throwing rocks up in the air, and one of them landed on my lawn. I put down the hose and yelled at him. What the hell did he think he was doing? He didn't have a chance to tell me. His sister ran up from somewhere behind him and started screaming in my face, calling me names and threatening me with destruction. She was wild with rage. This affected the dog, who advanced with fangs bared. He would have gone for me if she hadn't grabbed his collar. She called me another name, then seized her brother's hand and led him away.

The effect of this was that I fell a little in love with her. I was sorry when she moved away a few months later. The family had broken up, someone told me—nothing more detailed than that. I never knew her name. Over the next year or so I sometimes thought of her, wondered where she'd fetched up, how she was getting along. Out of these thoughts came the story "Coming Attractions."

I'd been writing another story altogether, based on an experience of my mother's when she worked in a movie theater. It didn't go anywhere until, for no reason, I began to see this girl in the story. I took my mother out, moved the theater from Seattle to California, changed the time to the present. Everything followed from that. I had her face before me, her movements, my sense of what she might be up to. And my idea of her began to evoke memories of kids I'd known when I was a high school teacher, and of myself when I was young—kids in the situation of being too much on their own, and forced to recognize, too soon, the unreliability of their parents and the whole shaky edifice of adult life. Thus the story grew in ways both general and particular, inventive and autobiographical.

And after it had passed through these complications, away from the girl who was its inspiration, the story led me back to her. I was sure that she was getting into all kinds of trouble, running wild, but at the same time I thought she might turn out all right in the end. She had a magnificent, almost insane capacity for love and loyalty. I had seen it. She thought of herself as responsible, and this vision of herself could give her the endurance, even heroism, her life would require.

Hence the ending. I don't know why I thought of that bicycle in the swimming pool. I once pulled one out, and it was hard, but how I came to put it in this girl's story is a mystery to me. A friend of mine said, "Oh, that's a baptismal scene, an image of purification and renewal."

Well, so be it. I'm glad to have arranged a baptism for her. I would like to think that she's in good hands.

Tobias Wolff

Selected Works by Tobias Wolff

Fiction

In the Garden of North American Martyrs. New York: Ecco Press, 1981.
The Barracks Thief. New York: Ecco Press, 1984.
Back in the World. Boston: Houghton Mifflin, 1985.

Other

This Boy's Life. New York: Atlantic Monthly Press, 1989.

Editor. *Matters of Life and Death: New American Stories.* Green Harbor: Wampeter, 1982.

Individual Interview

With Jean W. Ross. *Contemporary Authors*, 117. Detroit: Gale Research, 1987.

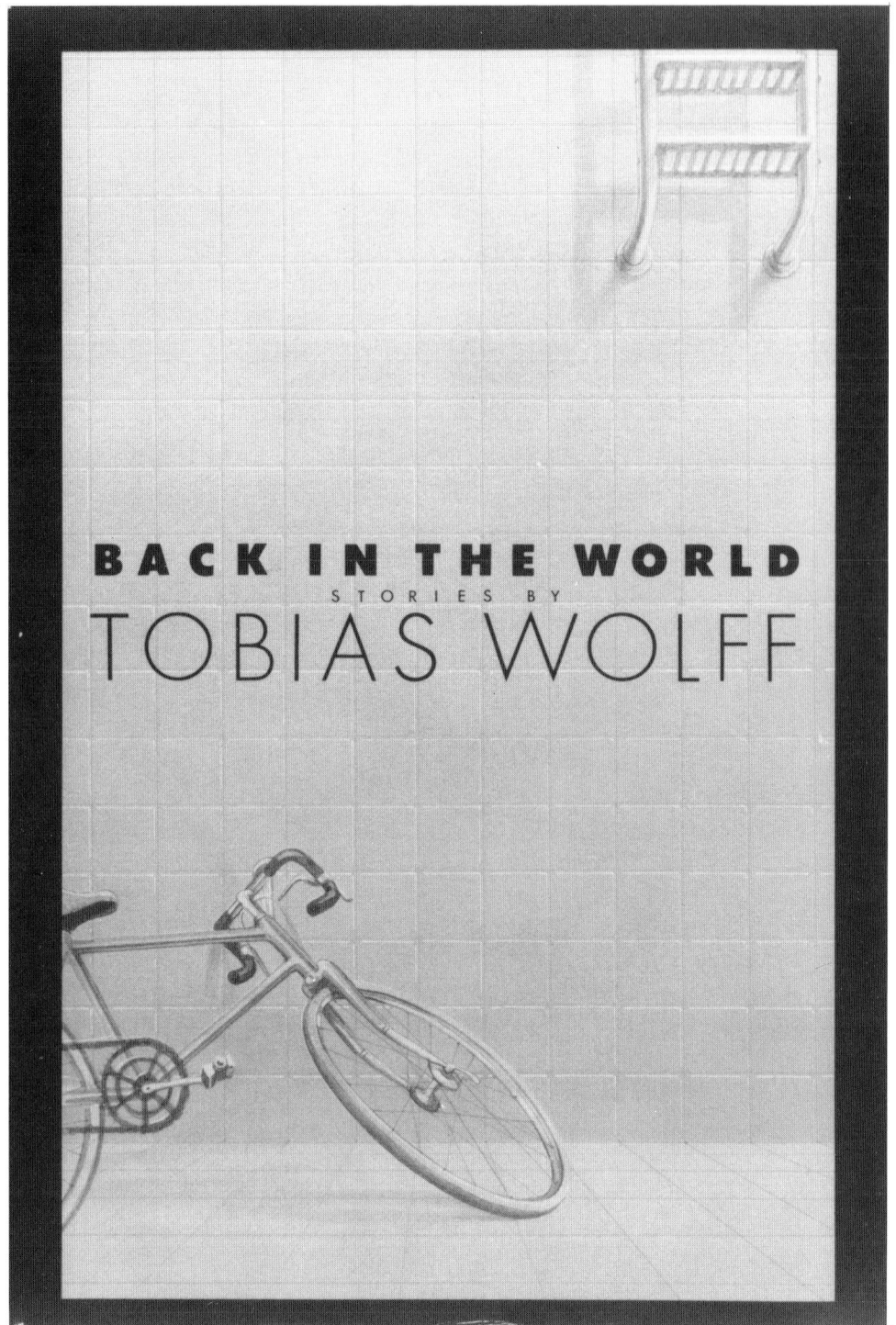

BACK IN THE WORLD
STORIES BY
TOBIAS WOLFF

Al Young

Al Young's career is a fascinating fusion of writing and music. Born in southern Mississippi in 1939, Young spent his early years in the rural South. Even after his family moved to Detroit in 1946, he returned every summer to his grandparents' home in Mississippi where, Young says, he "was surrounded by a powerful oral storytelling tradition." By the ninth grade he knew "that being a writer was...going to be my destiny."

Music was an equally strong part of Young's childhood. His father, a jazz musician until the family moved to Detroit, owned an extensive record collection. "Before I even knew how to distinguish different kinds of music," Young says, "I was subjected to a lot of music from the '20s, '30s, '40s, particularly jazz and generally Black American music—swing bands, the Ink Spots, Louis Jordan and His Tympany Five, all these people." Young also learned to read music and play the tuba, trumpet, and guitar. Later, while studying writing as an undergraduate at the University of Michigan, he supported himself as a free-lance musician. Upon graduation in 1961, Young went to work as a disc jockey for KJAZ-FM in Alameda, California. He stayed there until 1965, when he accepted a Stegner Fellowship and dedicated himself to writing. But even now, after nearly twenty-five years of writing, music continues to influence his style and subject matter.

Although Young's fellowship at Stanford was in fiction, his first book was a collection of poetry. Published in 1969, shortly before he returned to Stanford as a Jones Lecturer in Creative Writing, *Dancing* seeks to reproduce in language the universal appeal and emotional power of music. "Poetry should be a music of love," Young explains, a "song, a dance, the joyously heartbreaking flight of the human spirit through inner and outer space in search of itself." By celebrating the beauty that unites people of different ethnic groups, Young set himself apart from many of his black contemporaries, whose poetry militantly espoused a separate Afro-American culture. In Young's eyes, poetry should not promote a particular social agenda. Rather it should affirm the richness and diversity of all human experience. "For me, the most pleasant way of dealing with poetry is as language stripped of all its usual props. It isn't language that should necessarily fix you in a particular place or time or skin or culture or whatever." Since *Dancing*, Young has published two other books of poetry, which were collected with new verse in *The Blues Don't Change* (1982). In all his poems, Young invokes the familiar rhythms of boogie, blues, and jazz to emphasize a common ground of feeling. "I really try to do in poetry what musicians do with sound," he says, "which is just to stick within forms that people can follow, pat their feet to or hum or something like that and remember the melody afterwards—but within that little confining space to really try to talk about things."

A year after *Dancing*, Young published his first novel, *Snakes* (1970), which he had worked on during his year as a Stegner Fellow. Like his poetry, Young's fiction refuses the politics of racial conflict. Instead of projecting a homogeneous black society in polar opposition to white America, Young celebrates cultural diversity within the black community, highlighting the unique personalities of his characters as expressed in the rhythms of their language. "I found out early," he explains, "that speech is characterization. You can tell something about someone by the phrases they use repeatedly, the kinds of metaphors they come up with, how original they are or if they're just traditional things. It's one of the last manifestations of diversity in our culture." To reveal these subtle differences, Young's novels focus less on the socio-economic context of his characters' lives than on their personal ties to family and friends. *Snakes* carefully traces the development of M.C. Moore, a young man growing up in Detroit, who finds himself and his place in the world through his love of music. Playing electric guitar in a band, M.C. comes to respect different types of people by learning to appreciate the music of their speech. "I listen and look for it everywhere I go," says M.C., "in the streets, in the country, in people's voices, in their movements, in the way they lead their lives." Since *Snakes*, Young has published four other novels, including *Ask Me Now* (1980), described by Alan Cheuse in the *New York Times Book Review* as a "triumph of psychological insight and subtle narrative tones,...beautifully orchestrated, with every note and beat and nuance in place." His newest novel, *Seduction by Light* (1988), is already earning praise for its subversion of Hollywood stereotypes.

Not only has Young devoted his own art to celebrating diversity; he has also sought to open contemporary American letters to a greater range of ethnic voices. In 1972 Young joined with Ishmael Reed to create the multicultural periodical *Yardbird*. The title—Charlie Parker's nickname—was intended to signal the editors' commitment to artistic expression as free and eclectic as Parker's jazz. This publication's intention, says Young, was "to showcase fresh writing talent in a diversified setting that was singularly, if not subversively, multicultural like America herself." From the beginning until its demise in 1976, it included poetry, prose, and fiction by white, Asian, Afro-, Latin and Native American writers, including Ntozake Shange, Leslie Silko, Richard Kostelanetz, Victor Hernandez Cruz, and Simon Ortiz. Reed and Young continue to publish interracial literature in their periodical *Quilt*, which they have jointly edited since 1981.

But the major focus of Young's creative life in the 1980s has been a series of musical memoirs, *Bodies and Soul* (1981), *Kinds of Blue* (1984) and *Things Ain't What They Used to Be* (1987), in which he directly addresses the influence of music on his life and his art. The books are collections of short prose pieces elaborating Young's encounters with individual works of music. "Sometimes," Young says, "the remembering takes the form of story or personal myth. At other times the interaction between author and song or body of music gives birth to a related narrative or account, formal or informal, or a reverie, a fantasy or an inspired soliloquy." But unifying all this diversity is music's ability to cross cultural, racial, and temporal barriers. In one section Young describes a beach cabin in Asilomar, California, with Leroi Jones playing the Supremes' *Where Did Our Love Go?*; and in another, he recounts a performance of Gilbert and Sullivan's *The Mikado* in Dinkelspiel Auditorium on the Stanford campus. Although these two pieces of music could hardly be more different, for Young they are equally evocative of universal human feelings. The extremes of time, place, and cultural context fade into the background as the music fills Young's emotions and memories.

"Ideally," Thomas McGuane was asking me, "What would you like to get out of a writing career?"

Tom put that question to me when we met for the very first time upstairs in the old Jones Room of the Stanford Library. It was 1966, autumn, and we were both just past our middle 20's and elated about being there as Wallace Stegner Creative Writing Fellows.

"I'd be happy," I told him, thinking hard, "if I could one day support a family from writing."

"Is that all?"

"I think that'd be doing pretty well," I said.

"Not me," said Tom. "I want to be a tycoon!"

And this was how that wild, productive year got off the ground. The bright-eyed Fellows that time around included James D. Houston, Walt Alexander, Helena (Holly) Worthen, Louis Logan and, all the way from Australia, Peter Smart. Mary Jane Moffat was among those writers who were also enrolled in the graduate fiction-writing seminar, and there was Marshall Bremen, John McClusky, Mason Smith, Melinda Popham, Michael Leonard, Bruce Merry from England, and the visiting Ghanian short story writer and playwright, Anna Ata Aidoo. Morton Grosser would also make guest appearances. Yes, there was a lot of moveable feasting and partying, sometimes deep into the night. It was also the time when Flower Power, Sgt. Pepper's Lonelyhearts Club Band, the Black Panthers, Richard Brautigan's *Trout Fishing in America*, Eldridge Cleaver's *Soul on Ice*, anti-Vietnam War rallies, Love-Ins, Be-Ins and Right On! were rolling into vogue. In short, there was a heady, almighty anxiety quivering around the edges of everything that was going on just then, and it was oddly exhilarating. As an emerging poet and novelist who had spent years immersed in so-called underground culture, I found it refreshing to be passing through Stanford, where I could bob up for air.

Between the fall and spring of the 1966-67 academic year, I learned a great deal about the art and craft of fiction-writing from Wallace Stegner and Richard Scowcroft, who took turns conducting the seminar. Wally taught me that characterization and voice are, in themselves, powerful tools when it comes to building sound, solid dramatic narrative. Strong characterization and a rich, well-pitched voice can hold an entire book-length story together. Wally also taught me that what writers are really selling is energy and imagination.

What Dick Scowcroft taught me, in a nutshell, is this: If the action and events of a narrative serve to push it forward—that is, give the narrative movement—then you've got yourself a story. And if nothing happens in that narrative, then you might have a sketch or a vignette or even a prose-poem, but you ain't got no story. In stories stuff happens; people change, situations change; there is no standing still.

It was particularly important for me to hear these things again and again at a time when experimentalism and such concepts as anti-establishmentarianism and anti-story were bombarding literary circles; you might even say storming the Bastille of academicized art. I would liken myself to an impressionable young musician, a jazz player, say, who had only grown up with far-out avant-garde guidelines and no grounding whatever in an ongoing, older tradition. It was important to go back and practice scales and arpeggios in different keys, to get back down to fundamentals and basics in order to brighten and sharpen and deepen my own God-given voice.

When novelist Jessamyn West, or Irish short story master Sean O'Faolain or David Garnett ("My God," sighed McGuane, "he even knew Conrad!") dropped by to address our privileged little workshop, their prescriptive counsel and advice to novitiates predictably collided with what Gary Snyder or John Barth had to tell us. O'Faolain, for example, told us that we mustn't ever crowd a short story with any more than three characters. And poet Gary Snyder confided that when he taught a writing class, he and his students spent as little time as possible talking about

poetry or literature; rather, they went out and played a Japanese version of hopscotch he'd learned in Kyoto, or they would simply picnic or go for hikes or strolls along the beach. John Barth, of course, gave us the go-ahead by telling us it was OK, admirable, in fact, for fiction to be about fiction; for writing to be about writing.

Perhaps you've gotten the hang and feel of that amazing year by now. Dramatically invigorating is how I'd describe it. It wasn't unusual to find yourself involved in endless party-time sessions of the Deep-Talking-to-the-Deep with the likes of Ed McClanahan, Gurney Norman, John Hawkes (who was on campus working with Albert Guerard's unique approach to teaching freshman English: The Voice Project). And there was Jerome Charyn, Ron Shuman, Charlotte Painter or, resplendent in white suit and tie, Tom Wolfe, who was avidly trailing fugitive celebrity Ken Kesey around the Bay Area that year. *The Electric Kool-Aid Acid Test* is the book Wolfe penned from all that.

What an exciting time that was! The truth is that, as brash, aspiring, wet-behind-the-ears young writers, we all had some serious sprinting and long-distance running to do. For me, Stanford was a prominent, well-chalked starting-line, as it were.

From my writerly earnings, I've actually been able to support a small family, even though it has meant having to be highly versatile and prolific. And Thomas McGuane seems, indeed, to have become the tycoon he set out to be.

Al Young

Selected Works by Al Young

Fiction

Snakes. New York: Holt Rinehart, 1970.
Who Is Angelina? New York: Holt, Rinehart and Winston, 1975.
Sitting Pretty. New York: Holt, Rinehart and Winston, 1976.
Ask Me Now. New York: McGraw Hill, 1980.
Seduction by Light. New York: Dell, 1988.

Poetry

Dancing. New York: Corinth, 1969.
The Song Turning Back into Itself. New York: Holt, Rinehart and Winston, 1971.
Geography of the Near Past. New York: Holt, Rinehart and Winston, 1976.
The Blues Don't Change. Baton Rouge: Louisiana State University Press, 1982.

Other

Bodies and Soul. Berkeley: Creative Arts, 1981.
Kinds of Blue. Berkeley: Creative Arts, 1984.
Things Ain't What They Used to Be. Berkeley: Creative Arts, 1987.

Individual Interviews

"I Write the Blues: An Inteview with Al Young," with William J. Harris. *Greenfield Review*, Summer/Fall 1982.
"Interview with Al Young," with Nathaniel Mackey. *Melus*, Winter, 1978.

Recalling his year at Stanford as a Stegner Fellow, Al Young says, "Snakes was the novel I wrote during that crowded fellowship year. Let's put it another way: I wrote a version of a book called Snakes. After an editor at Viking named Aaron Asher told me that what I had were three stories, and that it would be necessary to select the one I truly wanted to tell, I sat down and completed the job." The story Young eventually chose to tell is about a young black musician coming of age in Detroit during the late 1950s and early 1960s. But Snakes did not fit the contemporary stereotypes of ethnic urban fiction. "The manuscript got turned down by editor after editor," Young explains, "one of whom said: 'A little too sweet for a ghetto novel.' As a black writer, then as now, you simply didn't cut ice commercially unless you were furious, poisonous or, at the very least, potentially dangerous. Because I was neither of the above, I knew even then that I would have to 'go the distance,' as James Baldwin once put it." In fact, Young published a book of poetry, a year before Holt Rinehart issued Snakes in 1970.

Al Young ⊘① SNAKES

        Our dreams went all the way back to junior high where
    we'd first met and begun to play together. Snakes started
    as bongo-type drummer who played on boxes and the bottoms
    of chairs. We met up in band where he came to take up reg-
    ular drums. I hadnt begun to play guitar yet. I was blow-
    ing tuba, or, rather, more properly, sousaphone, so we █████
    wound up next to each other way at the back of the band.
    Fuckups, Incorporated!
        I loved music and everything about it but never ███
    really expected to make any money out of it.
        Snakes, on the ██ other hand, never doubted for a moment
    that one day, if he stuck at it long enough, he would be a
    tycoon.
        When our record started climbing the charts and the
    first wave of money rolled in, the first thing he did was
    to have himself some new clothes tailored, put a down pay-
    ment on a Jaguar, move out of his folks' upstairs flat on the
    Clairmount, ████ where ███████████████████████ family
    had lived since coming up from Louisiana, ████████████████
    ███████ into a cozy little flashy modern apartment of his
    own on Boston Blvd. in the heart of Detroit's near northside.
    He couldnt understand me ████████ taking a room in the new
    house I'd started paying on for Claude, nor my general atti-
    tude about having a big record out. I wasnt exactly delighted.
        "I still dont understand you, MC. Here we are aint
    even old enough to vote yet and ██████ movin on up and you
    still runnin round here lookin distracted, and wanna be off
    by yourself and philosophizin and shit. ███████████████████
    ███████████████████████ Shoot, you better dig in on
    this good thing while it's happenin cause aint no tellin
    where it's gon lead to. Push come to shove, shit, we just
    might be back out in the streets before the year is out."

        I had been expecting a big magic moment to tick off
    ██████ at which time everything ████████████████████████████
    around me would fall into place, and everything about me
    would be transformed. That's the █████ least I had expected
    from success.
        All my life I have been confused. Very little ████
    ████████████ that I see ██ going on around me makes
    any sense. I dont know what people are doing. The only
    thing that has never ██████████████████████ let me down
    has been music -- not musicians, not promoters, club owners,
    recording companies, critics, reviwers. Music! I listen
    for it everywhere I go: not only in formal musical circum-
    stances or surroundings but everywhere -- in people's voices,
    in noises around me, in ███ other ████ fields even. A
    great painter sings to me; a fine poem sets my head vibrating
    with music; beautiful women arent melodies ████████████████
    ███████████████████ but █████ whole tone poems ███████
    ███████████████████, rich in line and full of deep feeling.
    I suppose you might say that I translate everything that
    I experience into music or look at the world from a musical
    point of view because that's the only way I can halfway get
    a bearing on what's going on. It's taken a while to be able

1.

        ⑧

    I see her feet on the floor in raggedy house slippers, legs spread
    quite thoughtlessly, enough to peek at the tops of her stockings
    beginning their roll just above the grayish knees.
    [South] Finally I keep trying to see myself emerging ████████ out of
    that shakey scene a homegrown nut, a peculiar lad who lived with
    his hard-working ████████ who ████████████ spends all her extra
    money playing the numbers, playing them hard. She wants to hit
    lucky and ease out of the game.
        When I was around eight or nine, Claude took sick and ███████
    didnt have the strength to look after me properly, so I was sent
    South to live with relatives -- Uncle Donald and Aunt Didi. They
    lived in Mississippi and were as poor as church mice the first year
    I spent with them. We lived in a rickety old frame house out from
    Meridian and had neckbones and rice for dinner everynight. Uncle
    Donald sold fruits and vegetables on the streets from ████ an ob-
    solescent truck and in ██ summer was the original watermelon man.
    There were █████ cousins in the country who supplied him with produce.
        Uncle Donald was also what they called a regular midnight ram-
    bler who drove his wife up walls the way he would lay out all night
    and keep up a █████████████ continued ruckus that involved other
    women, ████████ fights with other men working ████████████████
    ██████████████ out of the same bag. Wherever he went there was
    commotion. But he had a ████████████████████████ talent for get-
    ting hold of a dollar and dollars were scarce indeed. He bought an
    old used humpback Ford and had the legend BLACK JACK TAXI COMPANY
    stencilled on the side and drove around town up and down the streets
    picking up fares. After awhile, he got three or four other ████
    men to put the █████ Black Jack stamp on their cars and hustle pas-
    sengers as well, but there ███ was only so much money to be made
    off black people who took taxis in a small southern town.
        Uncle Donald started running whiskey for ████████████████
    ███ a black bootlegger who, alledgedly, was being backed by a white
    man whom some █████ people identified as the governor himself. With-
    in a year after I had come to live with them, quickly adjusting to
    the southern style of life and the funnytime public school system,
    Uncle Donald turned the house into a beer garden, a blind pig where
    people ████ slipped to have a few drinks, gamble, dance or just
    generally cut up and get their feet wet in the dry, dry state of
    Mississippi. The sheriff himself was often to be seen on the prem-
    ises, a black gal on either arm, loaded to his jowls that were red
    a lot and quivered when he put on his big white horselaugh.
        I ████ and my cousins -- ██ who were around the same age -- thought
    ██
    it was great to have a party going on all the time. We were ████████
    ████████████████████████████ regularly called in after the sun
    went down and playtime was over and hustled into a back bedroom from
    which we'd work our game of listening thru the walls, making number-
    less trips to the bathroom in order to get a peek at all the people
    & see all the fuss about the night, █████████████████████████
    ██████████████████████████
        Records would be playing, drinks poured, women and girls ████
    laughing ██████████████ and cackling ████████████ in high black
    tones and ████████ and registers. I used to sit with my cousin
    Jab by the wall next to the door and read comicbooks and dig all
    the sounds seeping thru. We'd █████ split a pack of BC Headache

2.

84 Al Young

1. Young composed this first draft of Snakes on the typewriter, revising as he wrote by "x"ing out words and phrases. After reviewing the draft in light of Asher's criticism, Young cut the first fifteen pages of the text, saving only the final paragraph on page seven, which he then expanded into the novel's opening. To formalize this change, Young wrote his name and the novel's title conspicuously across the top of his new first page and also renumbered the typescript by hand.

Young remarks that "music affects all of us in more powerful ways than we can measure…But I've noticed that with black people music really plays…a very strong role from early childhood in the way in which we see ourselves, the forming of our stylizations, the way we talk, all kinds of things." This idea is central to Snakes and is clearly present in the paragraph Young chooses as his opening. "I translate everything that I experience into music," says the book's adolescent narrator, and "look at the world from a musical point of view because that's the only way I can halfway get a bearing on what's going on."

2. Young revised his original typescript several times. Four separate sets of changes are indicated by the markings in black and red pencil and blue and red ink. In most of the changes, Young focuses on single words and phrases as they affect the cadences of the narrator's voice. "Listening to music, technically speaking, has taught me a great deal about the use of rhythm and silence in my writing," Young says, and here he refines these musical qualities of his language. The book's printed form is essentially identical to this revised first draft.

Permissions

Wendell Berry: photo © Dan Gillmor, reproduced by permission of Dan Gillmor; dust jacket of North Point Press edition of *Nathan Coulter*, reproduced by permission of North Point Press.

Edgar Bowers: photo by Learning Resources/Photographic Services, University of California, Santa Barbara; "The Court House" © 1987 Edgar Bowers, reprinted by permission of Edgar Bowers.

Raymond Carver: photo © Marion Ettlinger, reproduced by permission of Marion Ettlinger.

Evan S. Connell: photo © Thomas Victor, reproduced by permission of North Point Press; dust jacket of North Point Press edition of *Son of The Morning Star*, reproduced by permission of North Point Press.

Harriet Doerr: photo © Thomas Victor, reproduced by permission of Viking Press.

Ernest J. Gaines: photo by Bob Green, reproduced by permission of Ernest J. Gaines; dust jacket of *A Gathering of Old Men*, reproduced by permission of Alfred A. Knopf, Inc; page 10 of *A Gathering of Old Men* © 1985 Ernest J. Gaines, reprinted by permission of Alfred A. Knopf, Inc.

Thom Gunn: photo by Ander Gunn; reproduced by permission of Thom Gunn.

Donald Hall: photo by UNH Media Services, reproduced by permission of Donald Hall.

Robert Hass: photo © Barbara Hall; reproduced by permission of Ecco Press.

Donald Justice: photo reproduced by permission of Donald Justice.

Philip Levine: photo © Kelly Wise, reproduced by permission of Philip Levine; dust jacket of *A Walk with Tom Jefferson*, reprinted by permission of Alfred A. Knopf, Inc.;"Girl Help" reprinted by permission of Janet Lewis.

Thomas McGuane: photo by Paul Dix, reproduced by permission of Thomas McGuane.

Larry McMurtry: photo © Lee Marmon, reproduced by permission of Lee Marmon; dust jacket of *Horseman, Pass By*, reproduced by permission of Harper & Row, Inc; pages 158-159 of *Horseman, Pass By* © 1961 Larry McMurtry, reprinted by permission of Larry McMurtry.

N. Scott Momaday: photo reproduced by permission of N. Scott Momaday.

Tillie Olsen: photo reproduced by permission of Tillie Olsen.

Robert Pinsky: photo reproduced by permission of Robert Pinsky.

Alan Shapiro: photo by Patricia Evans, reproduced by permission of Alan Shapiro and Patricia Evans.

Scott Turow: photo © Tom Victor, reproduced by permission of Farrar Straus Giroux.

Tobias Wolff: photo © Jerry Bauer, reproduced by permission of Atlantic Monthly Press; dust jacket of *Back in the World* reproduced by permission of Fred Marcellino and Houghton Mifflin.

Al Young: photo © Jerry Bauer, reproduced by permission of Dell Publishing.

Printed and bound at Pinaire
Lithographing Corporation, Louisville,
Kentucky using Sterling Litho Matte
and Warren Patina.